Compact Guide to
Virginia
BIRDS

Curtis G. Smalling
Gregory Kennedy

LONE
PINE

Lone Pine Publishing International

The Distributor: Lone Pine Publishing
1808 B Street NW, Suite 140
Auburn, WA, USA 98001

Website: www.lonepinepublishing.com

Library and Archives Canada Cataloguing in Publication

Smalling, Curtis G., 1963-

    Compact guide to Virginia birds / Curtis G. Smalling, Gregory
Kennedy.

Includes bibliographical references and index.
ISBN-13: 978-976-8200-04-4
ISBN-10: 976-8200-04-9

1. Birds--Virginia--Identification. 2. Bird watching--Virginia. I.
Kennedy, Gregory, 1956- II. Title.

QL684.V8S63 2006   598'.09755   C2006-900001-8

Cover Illustration: Northern Cardinal by Gary Ross
Illustrations: Gary Ross, Ted Nordhagen, Eva Pluciennik
Egg Photography: Gary Whyte, Alan Bibby
Separations & Film: Elite Lithographers Co.

We wish to thank the Royal Alberta Museum for providing access to
their egg collection.

PC: 13

Contents

WATERFOWL

Snow Goose
size 32 in • p. 18

Canada Goose
size 42 in • p. 20

Tundra Swan
size 54 in • p. 22

Wood Duck
size 17 in • p. 24

Mallard
size 24 in • p. 26

Blue-winged Teal
size 15 in • p. 28

TURKEYS & QUAILS

Hooded Merganser
size 17 in • p. 30

Wild Turkey
size 39 in • p. 32

Northern Bobwhite
size 10 in • p. 34

DIVING BIRDS

Pied-billed Grebe
size 13 in • p. 36

Northern Gannet
size 36 in • p. 38

Double-crested Cormorant
size 29 in • p. 40

HERONS, IBISES & VULTURES

Great Blue Heron
size 51 in • p. 42

Great Egret
size 39 in • p. 44

Green Heron
size 18 in • p. 46

BIRDS OF PREY

Glossy Ibis
size 24 in • p. 48

Turkey Vulture
size 28 in • p. 50

Osprey
size 24 in • p. 52

Reference Guide 5

BIRDS OF PREY

Bald Eagle
size 36 in • p. 54

Sharp-shinned Hawk
size 12 in • p. 56

Red-tailed Hawk
size 21 in • p. 58

COOTS

American Kestrel
size 8 in • p. 60

American Coot
size 14 in • p. 62

Killdeer
size 10 in • p. 64

SHOREBIRDS

American Oystercatcher
size 18 in • p. 66

Lesser Yellowlegs
size 10 in • p. 68

Sanderling
size 8 in • p. 70

GULLS & TERNS

Laughing Gull
size 16 in • p. 72

Ring-billed Gull
size 19 in • p. 74

Great Black-backed Gull
size 30 in • p. 76

DOVES & CUCKOOS

Royal Tern
size 20 in • p. 78

Rock Pigeon
size 12 in • p. 80

Mourning Dove
size 12 in • p. 82

OWLS

Yellow-billed Cuckoo
size 12 in • p. 84

Eastern Screech-Owl
size 9 in • p. 86

Great Horned Owl
size 21 in • p. 88

OWLS

NIGHTJARS, SWIFTS & HUMMINGBIRDS

WOODPECKERS

FLYCATCHERS

SHRIKES & VIREOS

JAYS & CROWS

SWALLOWS

Barred Owl
size 20 in • p. 90

Whip-poor-will
size 9 in • p. 92

Chimney Swift
size 5 in • p. 94

Ruby-throated Hummingbird
size 4 in • p. 96

Belted Kingfisher
size 12 in • p. 98

Red-bellied Woodpecker
size 10 in • p. 100

Hairy Woodpecker
size 9 in • p. 102

Northern Flicker
size 12 in • p. 104

Pileated Woodpecker
size 16 in • p. 106

Eastern Phoebe
size 7 in • p. 108

Great Crested Flycatcher
size 9 in • p. 110

Eastern Kingbird
size 9 in • p. 112

Loggerhead Shrike
size 9 in • p. 114

Red-eyed Vireo
size 6 in • p. 116

Blue Jay
size 11 in • p. 118

American Crow
size 17 in • p. 120

Purple Martin
size 7 in • p. 122

Tree Swallow
size 5 in • p. 124

Barn Swallow
size 7 in • p. 126

Carolina Chickadee
size 5 in • p. 128

White-breasted Nuthatch
size 6 in • p. 130

Carolina Wren
size 5 in • p. 132

Eastern Bluebird
size 7 in • p. 134

Wood Thrush
size 8 in • p. 136

American Robin
size 10 in • p. 138

Gray Catbird
size 9 in • p. 140

Northern Mockingbird
size 10 in • p. 142

Brown Thrasher
size 11 in • p. 144

European Starling
size 8 in • p. 146

Cedar Waxwing
size 7 in • p. 148

Common Yellowthroat
size 5 in • p. 150

Pine Warbler
size 5 in • p. 152

Yellow-breasted Chat
size 8 in • p. 154

Scarlet Tanager
size 7 in • p. 156

Eastern Towhee
size 8 in • p. 158

Song Sparrow
size 6 in • p. 160

SWALLOWS

CHICKADEES, NUTHATCHES & WRENS

THRUSHES

MIMICS, STARLINGS & WAXWINGS

WOOD-WARBLERS & TANAGERS

SPARROWS & GROSBEAKS

SPARROWS, GROSBEAKS & BUNTINGS

White-throated Sparrow
size 7 in • p. 162

Dark-eyed Junco
size 6 in • p. 164

Northern Cardinal
size 8 in • p. 166

Blue Grosbeak
size 7 in • p. 168

Indigo Bunting
size 5 in • p. 170

Red-winged Blackbird
size 8 in • p. 172

BLACKBIRDS & ALLIES

Eastern Meadowlark
size 9 in • p. 174

Brown-headed Cowbird
size 7 in • p. 176

Baltimore Oriole
size 7 in • p. 178

FINCHLIKE BIRDS

American Goldfinch
size 5 in • p. 180

House Sparrow
size 6 in • p. 182

Introduction

If you have ever admired a songbird's pleasant notes, been fascinated by a soaring hawk or wondered how woodpeckers keep sawdust out of their nostrils, this book is for you. There is so much to discover about birds and their surroundings that birding is becoming one of the fastest growing hobbies on the planet. Many people find it relaxing, while others enjoy its outdoor appeal. Some people see it as a way to reconnect with nature, an opportunity to socialize with like-minded people or a way to monitor the environment.

Whether you are just beginning to take an interest in birds or can already identify many species, there is always more to learn. We've highlighted both the remarkable traits and the more typical behaviors displayed by some of our most abundant or noteworthy birds. A few live in specialized habitats, but most are common species that you have a good chance of encountering on most outings or in your backyard.

BIRDING IN VIRGINIA

We are truly blessed by the geographical and biological diversity of Virginia. In addition to supporting a wide range of breeding birds and year-round residents, our state hosts a large number of spring and fall migrants that move through our area on the way to their breeding and wintering grounds. In all, close to 400 bird species are regularly seen and recorded in Virginia and an additional 40 or so are rare or irregular.

Identifying birds in the wild and under varying conditions involves skill, timing and luck. The more you know about a bird—its range, preferred habitat, food preferences and hours and seasons of activity—the better your chances will be of seeing it. Generally, spring and fall are the busiest birding times.

Scarlet Tanager

Temperatures are moderate then, many species of birds are on the move, and in spring, male songbirds are belting out their unique courtship songs. Birds are usually most active in the early morning hours, except in winter, when they forage during the day when temperatures are milder.

Another useful clue for identifying birds is knowledge of their habitat. Simply put, a bird's habitat is the place where it normally lives. Some birds prefer open water, some birds are found in cattail marshes, others like mature coniferous forest, and still others prefer abandoned agricultural fields overgrown with tall grass and shrubs. Habitats are just like neighborhoods: if you associate friends with the suburb in which they live, you can easily learn to associate specific birds with their preferred habitats. Only in migration, especially during inclement weather, do some birds leave their usual habitat.

Virginia has a long tradition of friendly, recreational birding. In general, more experienced birders are willing to help beginners, share their knowledge and involve novices in their projects. Christmas bird counts, breeding bird surveys, nest box programs, migration monitoring and birding lectures and workshops provide a chance for birders of all levels to interact and share the splendor of birds. Bird hotlines provide up-to-date information on the sightings of rarities, which are often easier to relocate than you might think. For more information or to participate in these projects, contact the following organizations:

Red-winged Blackbird

Virginia Society of Ornithology
www.virginiabirds.net/

Virginia Audubon Council
www.cvco.org/science/vaudubon/

Virginia Birding and Wildlife Trail
Virginia Dept of Game and Inland Fisheries
4010 West Broad Street
PO Box 11104
Richmond, VA 23230-1104
www.dgif.va.us/

Rare Bird Alert
757-238-2713

BIRD LISTING

Many birders list the species they have seen during excursions or at home. It is up to you to decide what kind of list—systematic or casual—you will keep, and you may choose not to make lists at all. Lists may prove rewarding in unexpected ways, and after you visit a new area, your list becomes a souvenir of your experiences there. It can be interesting to compare the arrival dates and last sightings of hummingbirds and other seasonal visitors, or to note the first sighting of a new visitor to your area.

BIRD FEEDING

Many people set up bird feeders in their backyards, especially in winter. It is possible to attract specific birds by choosing the right kind of food and style of feeder. Keep your feeder stocked through late spring, because birds can have a hard time finding food before the flowers bloom, seeds develop and insects hatch. Contrary to popular opinion, birds do not become dependent on feeders, nor do they subsequently forget to forage naturally. Be sure to clean your feeder and the surrounding area regularly to prevent the spread of disease.

Landscaping your property with native plants is another way of providing natural food for birds. Flocks of waxwings have a keen eye for red mountain-ash berries and hummingbirds enjoy columbine flowers. The cumulative effects of "nature-scaping" urban yards can be a significant step toward habitat conservation (especially when you consider that habitat is often lost in small amounts—a power line is cut in one area and a highway is built in another). Many good books and web sites about attracting wildlife to your backyard are available.

NEST BOXES

Another popular way to attract birds is to put up nest boxes, especially for House Wrens, Eastern Bluebirds, Tree Swallows and Purple Martins. Not all birds will use nest boxes: only species that normally use cavities in trees are comfortable in such confined spaces. Larger nest boxes can attract kestrels, owls and cavity-nesting ducks.

Belted Kingfisher

ABOUT THE SPECIES ACCOUNTS

This book gives detailed accounts of 83 species of birds that can be expected in Virginia on an annual basis. The order of the birds and their common and scientific names follow the *American Ornithologists' Union Check-list of North American Birds* (7th edition, and its supplements through 2005).

As well as showing the identifying features of the bird, each species account also attempts to bring the bird to life by describing its various character traits. One of the challenges of birding is that many species look different in spring and summer than they do in fall and winter. Many birds have breeding and nonbreeding plumages, and immature birds often look different from their parents. This book does not try to describe or illustrate all the different plumages of a species; instead, it tries to focus on the forms that are most likely to be seen in our area.

ID: Large illustrations point out prominent field marks that will help you tell each bird apart. The descriptions favor easily understood language instead of technical terms.

Other ID: This section lists additional identifying features. Some of the most common anatomical features of birds are pointed out in the Glossary illustration (p. 185).

Size: The average length of the bird's body from bill to tail, as well as wingspan, are given and are approximate measurements of the bird as it is seen in nature. The size is sometimes given as a range,

Eastern Bluebird

because there is variation between individuals, or between males and females.

Voice: You will hear many birds, particularly songbirds, that may remain hidden from view. Memorable paraphrases of distinctive sounds will aid you in identifying a species by ear.

Status: A general comment such as "common," "uncommon" or "rare" is usually sufficient to describe the relative abundance of a species. Situations are bound to vary somewhat since migratory pulses, seasonal changes and centers of activity tend to concentrate or disperse birds.

Habitat: The habitats listed describe where each species is most commonly found. Because of the freedom flight gives them, birds can turn up in almost any type of habitat. However, they will usually be found in environments that provide the specific food, water, cover and, in some cases, nesting habitat they need to survive.

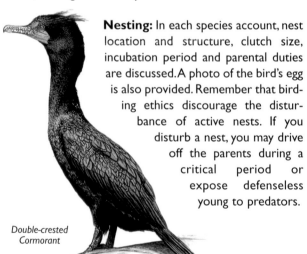

Nesting: In each species account, nest location and structure, clutch size, incubation period and parental duties are discussed. A photo of the bird's egg is also provided. Remember that birding ethics discourage the disturbance of active nests. If you disturb a nest, you may drive off the parents during a critical period or expose defenseless young to predators.

Double-crested Cormorant

Similar Birds: Easily confused species are illustrated for each account. If you concentrate on the most relevant field marks, the subtle differences between species can be reduced to easily identifiable traits. Even experienced birders can mistake one species for another.

Range Maps: The range map for each species shows the usual range of the species in an average year, but some birds wander beyond their traditional boundaries. The maps show breeding, summer and winter ranges, as well as migratory pathways—areas of the region where birds may appear while en route to nesting or winter habitat. The representations of the pathways do not distinguish high-use migration corridors from areas that are seldom used.

Range Map Symbols

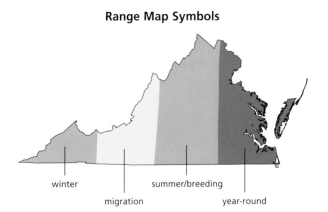

winter

migration

summer/breeding

year-round

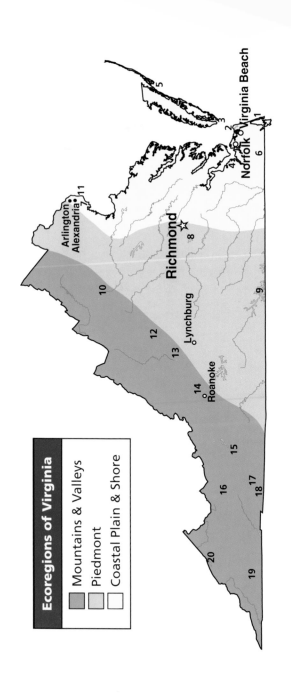

Ecoregions of Virginia

- Mountains & Valleys
- Piedmont
- Coastal Plain & Shore

Arlington
Alexandria
Richmond
Lynchburg
Roanoke
Norfolk
Virginia Beach

7
11
10
12
13
14
15
16
17
18
19
20
8
9
4
2
1
6
3
5

TOP BIRDING SITES

From the barrier islands off the Delmarva Peninsula and Chesapeake Bay to the breathtaking Shenandoah Mountains, our state can be separated into three natural regions: the Mountains and Valleys Region, the Piedmont, and the Coastal Plain and Shore (or Tidewater). Each region is composed of a number of different habitats that support a wealth of wildlife.

There are hundreds of good birding areas throughout our region The following areas have been selected to represent a broad range of bird communities and habitats, with an emphasis on accessibility.

1. Back Bay NWR
2. Chesapeake Bay Bridge-Tunnel
3. Kiptopeke SP
4. Hog Island WMA
5. Chincoteague NWR
6. Great Dismal Swamp NWR
7. Mason Neck SP and NWR
8. Pocahontas SP
9. John H. Kerr Reservoir
10. Shenandoah NP
11. Dyke Marsh
12. Blue Ridge Parkway
13. Warbler Road
14. Roanoke sewage treatment plant
15. Shot Tower Historical SP
16. Burkes Garden
17. Mount Rogers NRA
18. Grayson Highlands SP
19. Mendota fire tower
20. Breaks Interstate Park

NP - National Park
NRA - National Recreation Area
NWR - National Wildlife Refuge
SP - State Park
WMA - Wildlife Management Area

Snow Goose
Chen caerulescens

Noisy flocks of Snow Geese can be quite
entertaining, creating a moving patchwork in the
sky with their black wing tips and white plumage.
• These geese breed in the Arctic and northeastern
Siberia, crossing the Bering Strait twice a year.
Their smiling, serrated bills are made for grazing
on short arctic tundra plants and gripping the
slippery roots of marsh plants. • Snow Geese
can fly at speeds of up to 20 miles per hour.
They are also strong walkers and adults have been
known to lead their goslings up to 45 miles on foot
in search of suitable habitat.

Other ID: head often stained rusty red. *Blue
morph:* rare; white head and upper neck; dark blue-
gray body. *In flight:* black wing tips.
Size: L 30–33 in; W 4½–5 ft.
Voice: loud, nasal *houk-houk* in flight, higher
pitched and more constant than Canada Goose.
Status: common migrant in coastal regions; uncommon migrant inland in the Coastal Plain; locally
common winter resident around Chesapeake.
Habitat: croplands, fields, estuarine
marshes.

Similar Birds

Ross's Goose

Tundra Swan
(p. 22)

black wing tips

blue morph

dark "grin" on bill

Nesting: does not nest in Virginia; nests in the Arctic; female builds nest lined with grass, feathers and down; creamy white eggs are 3⅛ x 2 in; female incubates 4–7 eggs for 22–25 days.

Did You Know?

The Snow Goose has two color morphs, a white and a blue, which until 1983 were considered two different species.

Look For

Snow Geese fly in wavy, disorganized lines, whereas Canada Geese fly in V-formation. Occasionally mixed flocks form in migration.

Canada Goose
Branta canadensis

Canada Geese mate for life and are devoted parents. Unlike most birds, the family stays together for nearly a year, which increases the survival rate of the young. Rescuers who care for injured geese report that these birds readily adopt their human caregivers. However, wild geese can be aggressive, especially when defending young or competing for food. Hissing sounds and low, outstretched necks are signs that you should give these birds some space. • The Canada Goose was split into two species in 2004. The larger subspecies, including geese that breed in Virginia and the south-central states, are known as Canada Geese, while the smaller, arctic-breeding subspecies have been renamed Cackling Geese.

Other ID: dark brown upperparts; light brown underparts. *In flight:* flocks fly in V-formation.
Size: L 3–4 ft; W up to 6 ft.
Voice: loud, familiar *ah-honk*.
Status: common permanent resident statewide.
Habitat: lakeshores, riverbanks, ponds, farmlands and city parks.

Similar Birds

Cackling Goose

Brant

Greater White-fronted Goose

long, black neck

white "chin strap"

short, black tail

white undertail coverts

Nesting: usually on the ground; female builds a nest of grasses and mud, lined with down; white eggs are 3½ x 2¼ in; female incubates 3–8 eggs for 25–28 days.

Did You Know?

In Virginia, Canada Geese breed in March, and the first downy goslings of the year are normally seen in late April.

Look For

Geese graze on aquatic grasses and sprouts, and you can spot them tipping up to grab aquatic roots and tubers.

Tundra Swan
Cygnus columbianus

Magnificent Tundra Swans breed in the Arctic and winter along the East and West coasts. The eastern population overwinters mainly from the Carolinas northward. • These graceful birds are a long-lived species that mate for life. The young remain with their parents for their first winter in Virginia, and then the family flies back to the breeding grounds together. • The eastern population of Tundra Swans is estimated at over 100,000 birds and is climbing steadily. These birds traditionally fed on aquatic plants, but in recent years have taken a liking to more widely available waste grain in farm fields.

Other ID: slightly concave bill; black feet.
In flight: all-white wings.
Size: L 4–5 ft; W 6½ ft.
Voice: high-pitched, quivering *oo-oo-whoo,* repeated in flight.
Status: uncommon migrant inland in the Coastal Plain; common winter resident in Chesapeake region.
Habitat: shallow areas of lakes and wetlands, agricultural fields and flooded pastures.

Similar Birds

Snow Goose
(p. 18)

Ross's Goose

yellow lores

neck is held
straight up

Nesting: does not nest in Virginia; nests in the
Arctic; on an island or shoreline; nest is a large
mound of vegetation; creamy white eggs are
4¼ x 2⅜ in; female usually incubates 4–5 eggs
for 31–32 days.

Did You Know?

Tundra Swans take over
three months to migrate
from the Atlantic Coast to
the Arctic, but the swans
spend only about 120
hours in the air.

Look For

Tundra Swans and egrets
are our only completely
white birds. White Ibises,
Snow Geese and Northern
Gannets have black wing
tips, visible in flight.

Wood Duck
Aix sponsa

As their name implies, beautiful Wood Ducks are
forest-dwelling ducks, equipped with fairly sharp
claws for perching on branches and nesting in tree
cavities. • Female Wood Ducks often return to the
same nest site year after year, especially after successfully raising a brood. At these sites, the adults are
familiar with potential threats and have a better
chance keeping the nestlings safe. If Wood Ducks nest
in a local park or farmyard, do not approach
the nest, because fewer disturbances
increase the young's chance of survival.

Other ID: *Male:* glossy, green head with some white
streaks; white-spotted, purplish chestnut breast; dark
back and hindquarters. *Female:* gray-brown upperparts; white belly.
Size: L 15–20 in; W 30 in.
Voice: *Male:* ascending *ter-wee-wee. Female:* squeaky
woo-e-e-k.
Status: common migrant and locally common
breeder statewide; uncommon in winter.
Habitat: swamps, ponds, marshes and
lakeshores with wooded edges.

Similar Birds

Hooded Merganser
(p. 30)

Look For

A male Wood Duck defending
his mate from other interested
suitors will often strike an
interloper with an open wing
if one gets too close.

head raised in flight

white, teardrop-shaped eye patch

crest slicked back from crown

white "chin" and throat

golden sides

black and white shoulder slash

mottled brown breast streaked with white

Nesting: in a hollow, tree cavity or artificial nest box; usually near water; cavity is lined with down; white to buff eggs are 2⅛ x 1⅝ in; female incubates 9–14 eggs for 25–35 days.

Did You Know?

Newly hatched ducklings often jump 20 feet or more out of their nest cavities. Like downy ping-pong balls, they bounce on landing and are seldom injured.

Mallard
Anas platyrhynchos

The male Mallard, with his shiny green head and chestnut brown breast, is the classic wild duck. Mallards can be seen year-round, often in flocks and always near open water. These confident ducks have even been spotted dabbling in outdoor swimming pools. • Most people think of its quack as the typical duck call, but the Mallard is one of the only ducks that actually "quacks." • After breeding, male ducks lose their elaborate plumage, helping them stay camouflaged during their flightless period. In early fall, they molt back into breeding colors.

Other ID: orange feet. *Male:* white necklace; black tail feathers curl upward. *Female:* mottled brown overall.
Size: *L* 20–28 in; *W* 3 ft.
Voice: quacks; female is louder than male.
Status: common permanent resident statewide.
Habitat: lakes, wetlands, rivers, city parks, agricultural areas and sewage lagoons.

Similar Birds

Northern Shoveler

American Black Duck

Common Merganser

glossy, green head

yellow bill

dark blue speculum
bordered by white

♂

♀

orange bill
spattered
with black

Nesting: a grass nest is built on the ground or
under a bush; creamy, grayish or greenish white
eggs are 2¼ x 1⅝ in; female incubates 7–10 eggs
for 26–30 days.

Did You Know?

A nesting hen generates
enough body heat to
make the grass around
her nest grow faster. She
uses the tall grass to
further conceal her nest.

Look For

Mallards will readily hybridize
with a variety of other duck
species, often producing very
peculiar plumages.

Blue-winged Teal
Anas discors

Small, speedy Blue-winged Teals are renowned for their aviation skills. They can be identified by their small size and by the sharp twists and turns they execute in flight. • Blue-winged Teals and other dabbling ducks feed by tipping up their tails and dunking their heads underwater. Dabbling ducks have small feet situated near the center of their bodies. Other ducks such as scaup, scoters and Buffleheads dive underwater to feed, propelled by large feet set farther back on their bodies.

Other ID: broad, flat bill. *Male:* white undertail coverts. *Female:* mottled brown overall.
Size: L 14–16 in; W 23 in.
Voice: *Male:* soft *keck-keck-keck*. *Female:* soft quacks.
Status: common migrant statewide; uncommon winter resident at the coast.
Habitat: shallow lake edges and wetlands; prefers areas with short but dense emergent vegetation.

Similar Birds

Green-winged Teal

Northern Shoveler

green speculum

♀

♂

blue forewing patch

white throat

white crescent on face

blue-gray head

♀

♂

black-spotted breast and sides

Nesting: along a grassy shoreline or in a meadow; nest is built with grass and considerable amounts of down; whitish eggs are 1¾ x 1¼ in; female incubates 8–13 eggs for 23–27 days.

Did You Know?

Blue-winged Teals migrate farther than most ducks. They summer as far north as the Canadian tundra and overwinter mainly in Central and South America.

Look For

The male Blue-winged Teal's white crescent patch next to his bill is visible year-round.

Hooded Merganser
Lophodytes cucullatus

Extremely attractive and exceptionally shy, the male Hooded Merganser is one of the most sought-after ducks from a birder's perspective. Much of the time, the drake holds his crest flat, but in moments of arousal or agitation, he quickly unfolds his brilliant crest to attract a mate or to signal approaching danger. The drake displays his full range of colors and athletic abilities in elaborate, late-winter courtship displays and chases.

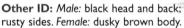

Other ID: *Male:* black head and back; rusty sides. *Female:* dusky brown body.
Size: *L* 16–18 in; *W* 24 in.
Voice: usually silent in winter; low grunts and croaks. *Male:* froglike *crrrrooo* in courtship display. *Female:* occasionally a harsh *gak* or a croaking *croo-croo-crook*.
Status: uncommon to common migrant over much of the state; uncommon winter resident but more common near the coast.
Habitat: forest-edged ponds, wetlands, lakes and rivers.

Similar Birds

Bufflehead

Red-breasted Merganser

Common Merganser

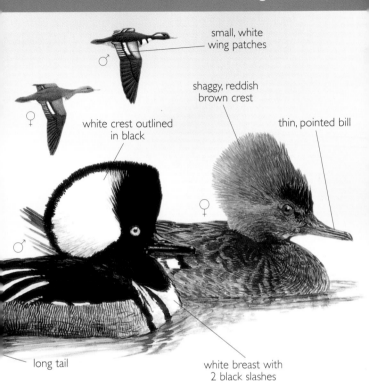

small, white wing patches

shaggy, reddish brown crest

white crest outlined in black

thin, pointed bill

♂ ♀

long tail

white breast with 2 black slashes

Nesting: a few nesting records for coastal Virginia; nests in northwestern and northeastern U.S. and Canada; usually in a tree cavity lined with leaves and down; white eggs are 2¼ x 1¾ in; female incubates 10–12 eggs for 29–33 days.

Did You Know?

All mergansers have serrated bills for grasping slippery fish. Unlike other mergansers, Hoodies also add crustaceans, insects and acorns to their diet.

Look For

The Hooded Merganser has a long tail that is often held erect while swimming.

Wild Turkey
Meleagris gallopavo

The Wild Turkey was once common throughout most of eastern North America, but in the 20th century, habitat loss and overhunting took a toll on this bird. Today, efforts at restoration have reestablished the Wild Turkey nearly statewide. • This charismatic bird is the only native North American animal that has been widely domesticated. • Early in life both male and female turkeys gobble. The females eventually outgrow this practice, leaving males to gobble competitively for the honor of mating.

Other ID: largely unfeathered legs. *Male:* red wattles; black-tipped breast feathers. *Female:* smaller; blue-gray head; less iridescent plumage; brown-tipped breast feathers.
Size: *Male:* L 3–3½ ft; W 5½ ft. *Female:* L 3 ft; W 4 ft.
Voice: wide array of sounds; courting male gobbles loudly; alarm call is a loud *pert;* gathering call is a cluck; contact call is a loud *keouk-keouk-keouk.*
Status: common to uncommon permanent resident statewide.
Habitat: deciduous, mixed and riparian woodlands; occasionally eats waste grain and corn in late fall and winter.

Similar Birds

Ring-necked Pheasant

Look For

Eastern Wild Turkeys have brown or rusty tail tips and are slimmer than domestic turkeys, which have white tail tips.

naked, blue-red head

barred, copper-colored tail

dark glossy, iridescent body plumage

long central breast tassel

♂

Nesting: under thick cover in a woodland or at a field edge; nests on ground in a depression lined with vegetation; brown-speckled, pale buff eggs are 2½ x 1¾ in; female incubates 10–12 eggs for up to 28 days.

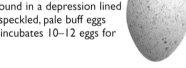

Did You Know?

If Congress had taken Benjamin Franklin's advice in 1782, our national emblem would be the Wild Turkey instead of the majestic Bald Eagle.

Northern Bobwhite
Colinus virginianus

In spring, the characteristic, whistled *bob-white* call of our only native quail is heard across Virginia. The male's well-known call is often the only evidence of its presence among the dense, tangled vegetation of its rural, woodland home. • Throughout fall and winter, Northern Bobwhites typically travel in large family groups called coveys. When a predator approaches, the covey bursts into flight, creating a confusing flurry of activity. With the arrival of summer, breeding pairs break away from their coveys to perform elaborate courtship rituals in preparation for another nesting season.

Other ID: mottled brown, buff and black upperparts; white crescents and spots edged in black on chestnut brown sides and upper breast; short tail.
Size: *L* 10 in; *W* 13 in.
Voice: whistled *hoy* is given year-round. *Male:* a whistled, rising *bob-white* in spring and summer.
Status: uncommon permanent resident statewide.
Habitat: farmlands, open woodlands, woodland edges, grassy fencelines, roadside ditches and brushy, open country.

Similar Birds

Ruffed Grouse

Look For

Bobwhites benefit from habitat disturbance and are often found in early succession habitats created by fire, agriculture and forestry.

broad, white "eyebrow"

buff throat and "eyebrow"

white throat

♀

♂

rufous breast

Nesting: in a shallow depression on the ground, often concealed by vegetation or a woven, partial dome; nest is lined with grass and leaves; white to pale buff eggs are 1¼ x 1 in; pair incubates 12–16 eggs for 22–24 days.

Did You Know?

Northern Bobwhites huddle together on cold winter nights, with each bird facing outward, enabling the group to detect danger from any direction.

Pied-billed Grebe
Podilymbus podiceps

Relatively solid bones and the ability to partially deflate its air sac allow the Pied-billed Grebe to sink below the surface of the water like a tiny submarine.

nonbreeding

These birds tend to stick to the shallow waters of quiet bays and rivers, where they can disappear into the cattails without leaving a trace. • While a few Pied-billed Grebes can be found year-round in Virginia, they are most common from September to May, when solitary individuals are often seen on larger rivers and lakes near the coast.

Other ID: *Breeding:* all-brown body; laterally compressed bill; white undertail coverts; pale belly. *Nonbreeding:* yellow bill lacks black ring; white "chin" and throat; brownish crown.
Size: *L* 12–15 in; *W* 16 in.
Voice: loud, whooping call begins quickly, then slows down: *kuk-kuk-kuk cow cow cow cowp cowp cowp.*
Status: common statewide in migration and winter; occasional breeding records.
Habitat: ponds, marshes and backwaters with sparse emergent vegetation.

Similar Birds

American Coot
(p. 62)

Horned Grebe

dark eye with pale ring

black ring on pale bill

very short tail

black throat

breeding

Nesting: a few breeding records from across the state; in a wetland; floating platform nest of decaying plants is anchored to emergent vegetation; white to buff eggs are 1⅝ x 1¼ in; pair incubates 4–5 eggs for about 23 days and raises the striped young together.

Did You Know?

When frightened by an intruder, these grebes cover their eggs and slide underwater, leaving a nest that looks like nothing more than a mat of debris.

Look For

Its dark plumage, individually webbed toes and chickenlike bill distinguish the Pied-billed Grebe from other waterfowl.

Northern Gannet
Morus bassanus

The Northern Gannet, with its elegant "mask" and high forehead, slices through the open ocean air with blackened wing tips. This gentle-looking bird mates for life and does not breed until it is at least five years old. Pair bonds are reestablished each year with elaborate face-to-face rituals that include wing raising, tail spreading, bowing and preening. The female lays a single egg, which she incubates under the webs of her feet.

Other ID: white overall; long, narrow wings; pointed tail; black feet. *In flight:* black wing tips.
Size: L 3–3¼ ft; W 6 ft.
Voice: usually silent at sea; feeding flocks may exchange grating growls.
Status: common migrant and winter resident offshore and nearshore on the coast and in Chesapeake Bay.
Habitat: roosts and feeds in open ocean waters most of the year; often seen well offshore; regularly seen inshore during migration.

Similar Birds

Snow Goose
(p. 18)

Look For

Squadrons of gannets soaring at more than 100 feet above the ocean will suddenly fold their wings back and plunge headfirst into the water in pursuit of schooling fish.

juvenile

buffy wash on nape

thick, tapered,
pale gray bill

black wing tips

Nesting: does not nest in Virginia; nests on protected mainland or island sea cliffs from Maine
northward; male builds a tall mound of seaweed
and other debris; pale blue to white egg is 3 x 2 in;
pair shares incubation of 1 egg.

Did You Know?

Gannets are pelagic birds that spend months at sea, sometimes
resting on the water but rarely landing on solid earth except
to nest.

Double-crested Cormorant

Phalacrocorax auritus

The Double-crested Cormorant looks like a bird but smells and swims like a fish. With a long, rudderlike tail and excellent underwater vision, this slick-feathered bird has mastered the under-water world. Most waterbirds have waterproof feathers, but the structure of the cormorant's feathers allow water in. "Wettable" feathers make this bird less buoyant, which in turn makes it a better diver. The Double-crested Cormorant also has sealed nostrils for diving and must fly with its bill open to breathe.

Other ID: all-black body; blue eyes. *Immature:* brown upperparts; buff throat and breast; yellowish throat patch. *In flight:* rapid wingbeats; kinked neck.
Size: L 26–32 in; W 4¼ ft.
Voice: generally quiet; may issue piglike grunts or croaks, especially near nest colonies.
Status: uncommon but increasing breeder; common to abundant migrant statewide; winter resident in the Coastal Plain.
Habitat: large lakes and large, meandering rivers.

Similar Birds

Great Cormorant

Common Loon

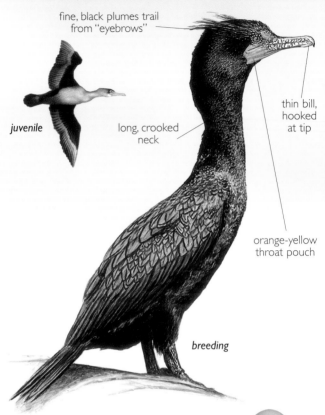

fine, black plumes trail from "eyebrows"

juvenile

long, crooked neck

thin bill, hooked at tip

orange-yellow throat pouch

breeding

Nesting: a few breeding locations in Virginia coastal region; colonial; on an island or high in a tree; platform nest is made of sticks and guano; pale blue eggs are 2 x 1½ in; pair incubates 2–7 eggs for 25–30 days.

Did You Know?

Japanese fishermen sometimes use cormorants on leashes to catch fish. This traditional method of fishing is called *Ukai.*

Look For

Double-crested Cormorants often perch on trees or piers with their wings partially spread to dry their feathers and regulate body temperature.

Great Blue Heron
Ardea herodias

The long-legged Great Blue Heron has a stealthy, often-motionless hunting strategy. It waits for a fish or frog to approach, spears the prey with its bill, then flips its catch into the air and swallows it whole. Herons usually hunt near water, but they also stalk fields and meadows in search of rodents.
• Great Blue Herons settle in communal treetop nests called rookeries. Nesting herons are sensitive to human disturbance, so observe this bird's behavior from a distance.

Other ID: blue-gray overall; long, dark legs. *Breeding:* richer colors; plumes streak from crown and throat. *In flight:* black upperwing tips; legs trail behind body; slow, steady wingbeats.
Size: L 4¼–4½ ft; W 6 ft.
Voice: quiet away from the nest; occasional harsh *frahnk frahnk frahnk* during takeoff.
Status: common permanent resident statewide; uncommon in winter in the mountains.
Habitat: forages along edges of rivers, lakes and marshes; also fields and wet meadows.

Similar Birds

Little Blue Heron

Black-crowned
Night-Heron

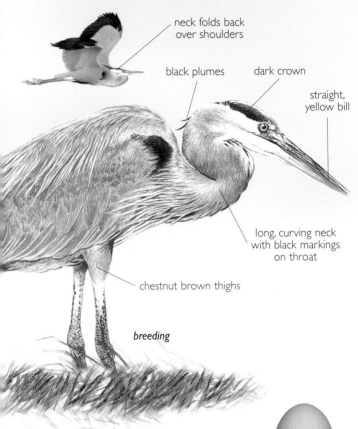

neck folds back over shoulders

black plumes

dark crown

straight, yellow bill

long, curving neck with black markings on throat

chestnut brown thighs

breeding

Nesting: colonial; adds to stick platform nest over years; nest width can reach 4 ft; pale bluish green eggs are 2½ x 1¾ in; pair incubates 4–7 eggs for approximately 28 days.

Did You Know?

The Great Blue Heron is the tallest of all the herons and egrets in North America.

Look For

In flight, the Great Blue Heron folds its neck back over its shoulders in an S-shape. Similar-looking cranes stretch their necks out when flying.

Great Egret
Ardea alba

The plumes of the Great Egret and Snowy Egret (*Egretta thula*) were widely used to decorate hats in the early 20th century. An ounce of egret feathers cost as much as $32—more than an ounce of gold at that time—and, as a result, egret populations began to disappear. Some of the first conservation legislation in North America was enacted to outlaw the hunting of Great Egrets. We recently celebrated the 100th anniversary of the nation's first National Wildlife Refuge, Pelican Island in Florida. Established by Teddy Roosevelt in 1903, the refuge set aside a small island where it was illegal to hunt egrets for the feather trade.

Other ID: long, all-white plumage. *In flight:* legs extend backward.
Size: L 3–3½ ft; W 4 ft.
Voice: rapid, low-pitched, loud *cuk-cuk-cuk*.
Status: common breeder and migrant in the coastal region, becoming less common to absent in winter; uncommon migrant inland.
Habitat: marshes, open riverbanks, irrigation canals and lakeshores.

Similar Birds

Snowy Egret

Cattle Egret

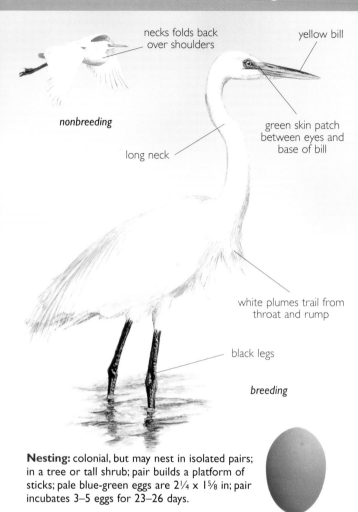

necks folds back over shoulders

yellow bill

nonbreeding

green skin patch between eyes and base of bill

long neck

white plumes trail from throat and rump

black legs

breeding

Nesting: colonial, but may nest in isolated pairs; in a tree or tall shrub; pair builds a platform of sticks; pale blue-green eggs are 2¼ x 1⅝ in; pair incubates 3–5 eggs for 23–26 days.

Did You Know?

The Great Egret is the symbol for the National Audubon Society, one of the oldest conservation organizations in the United States.

Look For

Great Egrets are named for their impressive breeding plumes, or "aigrettes," which can grow up to 4½ feet long!

Green Heron
Butorides virescens

Sentinel of mangroves and marshes, the ever-vigilant Green Heron sits hunched on a shaded branch at the water's edge. This crow-sized heron stalks frogs and small fish lurking in the weedy shallows, then stabs prey with its bill. • Unlike most herons, the Green Heron nests singly rather than communally, although it can sometimes be found in loose colonies. While some of this heron's habitat has been lost to wetland drainage or channelization in the southern states, the building of farm ponds or reservoirs has created habitat in other areas.

Other ID: stocky body; relatively short, yellow-green legs; long bill is dark above and greenish below; short tail. *Breeding male:* bright orange legs.
Size: L 15–22 in; W 26 in.
Voice: generally silent; alarm and flight call are a loud *kowp, kyow* or *skow*; aggression call is a harsh *raah*.
Status: fairly common breeder statewide; rare in winter at the coast.
Habitat: marshes, lakes and streams with dense shoreline or emergent vegetation; mangroves.

Similar Birds

Black-crowned
Night-Heron

Least Bittern

American Bittern

dark, iridescent back

green-black crown

chestnut face and neck

Nesting: nests singly or in small, loose groups; stick platform is built in a tree or shrub, usually close to water; blue-green to green eggs are 1½ x 1⅛ in; pair incubates 3–5 pale eggs for 19–21 days.

Did You Know?

Green Herons have been seen baiting fish to the surface by dropping small bits of debris such as twigs, vegetation or feathers into the water.

Look For

The scientific name *virescens* is Latin for "growing or becoming green" and refers to this bird's transition from a streaky brown juvenile to a greenish adult.

Glossy Ibis

Plegadis falcinellus

The exotic look of the Glossy Ibis hints at its distant West Africa origins. The same powerful trade winds that drew Christopher Columbus to North America may also have guided these graceful birds to the warm, productive Caribbean only a few centuries ago. In the 1930s, the Glossy Ibis established a small breeding colony in the rich coastal marshes of Florida, then quickly expanded its range up the East Coast. Sporadic breeding records along the coast of Maine and southeastern Canada suggest that the population will continue to expand northward.

Other ID: *Breeding:* chestnut head, neck and sides; green and purple sheen on wings, tail, crown and face. *Nonbreeding:* dark grayish-brown head and neck are streaked with white. *In flight:* hunchbacked appearance; legs trail behind tail.
Size: *L* 22–25 in; *W* 3 ft.
Voice: cooing accompanies billing and preening during nest relief.
Status: common summer resident in coastal marshes; uncommon migrant inland; uncommon in winter at the coast.
Habitat: marshes, swamps, flooded fields and shallow estuaries with adequate shoreline vegetation for nesting.

Similar Birds

White Ibis   Little Blue Heron

long, downcurved bill

nonbreeding

dark skin in front of brown eye is bordered by 2 pale stripes

breeding

long legs

Nesting: in a colony, often with egret and heron rookeries; bulky platform of marsh vegetation and sticks is built over water, on the ground or on top of tall shrubs or small trees; pale blue or green eggs are 2 x 1½ in; pair incubates 2–4 eggs for approximately 21 days.

Did You Know?

The Glossy Ibis sweeps its head back and forth through the water or uses its long bill to probe the marshland mud for unseen prey.

Look For

Flocks of Glossy Ibis fly in lines or V-formation, and individuals hold their neck fully extended in flight.

Turkey Vulture

Cathartes aura

Turkey Vultures are intelligent, playful and social birds. Groups live and sleep together in large trees, or "roosts." Some roost sites are over a century old and have been used by the same family for several generations. • The genus name *Cathartes* means "cleanser" and refers to this bird's affinity for carrion. Its red, featherless head may appear grotesque, but this adaptation allows it to stay relatively clean while feeding on messy carcasses. • No other bird uses updrafts and thermals in flight as well as the Turkey Vulture. Pilots have reported seeing vultures soaring at 20,000 feet.

Other ID: *Immature:* gray head. *In flight:* head appears small; rocks from side to side when soaring.
Size: L 25–31 in; W 5½–6 ft.
Voice: generally silent; occasionally produces a hiss or grunt if threatened.
Status: common permanent resident statewide.
Habitat: usually flies over open country, shorelines or roads; rarely over forests.

Similar Birds

Black Vulture

Golden Eagle

Bald Eagle
(p. 54)

silver gray flight feathers

holds wing in a shallow "V"

bare, red head

brownish black overall

pale, hooked bill

Nesting: in a cave, crevice, log or among boulders; uses no nest material; dull white eggs, irregularly marked with brown and purple, are 2¾ x 2 in; pair incubates 2 eggs for up to 41 days.

Did You Know?

A threatened Turkey Vulture will play dead or throw up. The odor of its vomit repulses attackers, much like the odor of a skunk's spray.

Look For

Turkey Vultures often hop or run along the ground, especially when competing for a carcass.

Osprey
Pandion haliaetus

The large, powerful Osprey is almost always found near water. While hunting for fish, this bird hovers in the air before hurling itself in a dramatic headfirst dive. An instant before striking the water, it rights itself and thrusts its feet forward to grasp its quarry. The Osprey has specialized feet for gripping slippery prey—two toes point forward, two point backward and all are covered with sharp spines. • The Osprey is one of the most widely distributed birds in the world—it is found on every continent except Antarctica.

Other ID: yellow eyes; pale crown. *Male:* all-white throat. *Female:* fine, dark "necklace." *In flight:* long wings are held in a shallow "M"; brown and white tail bands.
Size: *L* 22–25 in; *W* 5½–6 ft.
Voice: series of melodious ascending whistles: *chewk-chewk-chewk;* also a familiar *kip-kip-kip.*
Status: common migrant and breeder at the coast; common to uncommon migrant inland.
Habitat: lakes and slow-flowing rivers and streams; estuaries and bays in migration.

Similar Birds

Bald Eagle (p. 54)

Rough-legged Hawk

dark eye line

dark "wrist" patches

gray bill

gray feet

long wings extend past tail

Nesting: on a treetop or artificial structure, usually near water; massive stick nest is reused annually; brown-blotched, yellowish eggs are 2⅜ x 1¾ in; pair incubates 2–4 eggs for 38 days.

Did You Know?

The Osprey's dark eye line blocks the glare of the sun on the water, enabling the bird to spot fish near the water's surface.

Look For

Ospreys build bulky nests on high, artificial structures such as communication towers and utility poles, or on buoys and channel markers over water.

Bald Eagle

Haliaeetus leucocephalus

This majestic sea eagle hunts mostly fish and is often found near water. While soaring hundreds of feet high in the air, an eagle can spot fish swimming underwater . Eagles also scavenge carrion and often steal food from other birds. • Bald Eagles do not mature until their fourth or fifth year— only then do they develop the characteristic white head and tail plumage.

Other ID: *1st-year:* dark overall; dark bill; some white in underwings. *2nd-year:* dark "bib"; white in underwings. *3rd-year:* mostly white plumage; yellow at base of bill; yellow eyes. *4th-year:* light head with dark facial streak; variable pale and dark plumage; yellow bill; paler eyes.
Size: L 30–43 in; W 5½–8 ft.
Voice: thin, weak squeal or gull-like cackle: *kleek-kik-kik-kik* or *kah-kah-kah*.
Status: threatened: uncommon breeder in the Coastal Plain and Piedmont; uncommon migrant statewide; uncommon winter resident in Cheasapeake and major rivers and reservoirs.
Habitat: seacoasts, estuaries, large lakes and rivers.

Similar Birds

Golden Eagle

Osprey (p. 52)

white head and tail

yellow bill

yellow feet

Nesting: in a tree; usually, but not always, near water; huge stick nest is often reused for many years; white eggs are 2¾ x 2⅛ in; pair incubates 1–3 eggs for 34–36 days.

Did You Know?

The Bald Eagle, a symbol of freedom, longevity and strength, became the emblem of the United States in 1782.

Look For

Bald Eagles mate for life and renew pair bonds by adding sticks to their nests, which can be up to 15 feet in diameter, the largest of any North American bird.

Sharp-shinned Hawk

Accipiter striatus

After a successful hunt, the small Sharp-shinned Hawk often perches on a favorite "plucking post" with its meal grasped in its razor-sharp talons. This hawk is a member of the *Accipter* genus, or wood-land hawks, and it preys almost exclusively on small birds. Its short, rounded wings, long, rudderlike tail and flap-and-glide flight allow it to maneuver through forests at high speed. • When delivering food to his nestlings, a male Sharp-shinned Hawk takes care not to disturb his mate—she is typically one-third larger than he is and notoriously short-tempered.

Other ID: *In flight:* short, rounded wings; dark barring on flight feathers.
Size: *Male: L 10–12 in; W 20–24 in. Female: L 12–14 in; W 24–28 in.*
Voice: usually silent; intense, repeated *kik-kik-kik-kik* during the breeding season.
Status: uncommon breeder in the mountains and Piedmont; common migrant statewide; uncommon winter resident.
Habitat: dense to semi-open forests and large woodlots; occasionally along rivers and in urban areas; favors bogs and dense, moist, coniferous forests for nesting.

Similar Birds

Cooper's Hawk

American Kestrel
(p. 60)

Merlin

red eyes

blue-gray crown,
back and upperwings

immature

red horizontal bars
on underparts

heavily barred,
square-tipped tail

Nesting: in a conifer; builds a new stick nest or uses an abandoned crow nest; brown-blotched, bluish white eggs are 1½ x 1⅛ in; female incubates 4–5 eggs for 34–35 days; male feeds the female during incubation.

Did You Know?

As it ages, the Sharp-shinned Hawk's bright yellow eyes become red. This change may signal full maturity to potential mates.

Look For

During winter, Sharp-shinned Hawks may visit backyard bird feeders to prey on feeding sparrows and finches. Watch for their flap-and-glide flight pattern.

Red-tailed Hawk
Buteo jamaicensis

Take an afternoon drive through the country and look for Red-tailed Hawks soaring above the fields. They are the most common hawks in Virginia, especially in winter. • In warm weather, these hawks use thermals and updrafts to soar. The pockets of rising air provide substantial lift, which allows migrating hawks to fly for almost 2 miles without flapping their wings. On cooler days, resident Red-tails perch on exposed tree limbs, fence posts or utility poles to scan for prey.

Other ID: brown eyes; overall color varies geographically. *In flight:* light underwing flight feathers with faint barring; dark leading edge on underside of wing; fan-shaped tail.
Size: *Male: L* 18–23 in; W 4–5 ft. *Female: L* 20–25 in; W 4–5 ft.
Voice: powerful, descending scream: *keeearrrr.*
Status: common year-round statewide.
Habitat: open country with some trees; also roadsides or woodlots.

Similar Birds

Rough-legged Hawk

Broad-winged Hawk

Red-shouldered Hawk

dark "shoulder" patches

dark upperparts with some white highlights

dark brown band of streaks across belly

red tail

Nesting: in woodlands adjacent to open habitat; bulky stick nest is enlarged each year; brown-blotched, whitish eggs are 2⅜ x 1⅞ in; pair incubates 2–4 eggs for 28–35 days.

Did You Know?

The Red-tailed Hawk's piercing call is often paired with the image of an eagle in TV commercials and movies.

Look For

Courting pairs will dive at each other, lock talons and tumble toward the earth, breaking away at the last second to avoid crashing into the ground.

American Kestrel
Falco sparverius

The colorful American Kestrel, formerly known as the "Sparrow Hawk," is a common and widespread falcon, not shy of human activity and adaptable to habitat change. This small falcon has benefited from the grassy right-of-ways created by interstate highways, which provide habitat for grasshoppers and other small prey. Watch for this robin-sized bird along rural roadways, perched on poles and telephone wires or hovering over agricultural fields, foraging for insects and small mammals.

Other ID: lightly spotted underparts. *In flight:* frequently hovers; buoyant, indirect flight style.
Size: L 7½–8 in; W 20–24 in.
Voice: usually silent; loud, often repeated, shrill *killy-killy-killy* when excited; female's voice is lower pitched.
Status: uncommon breeder statewide; common migrant (especially at the coast) and winter resident statewide.
Habitat: open fields, riparian woodlands, woodlots, forest edges, bogs, roadside ditches, grassy highway medians and croplands.

Similar Birds

Merlin

Sharp-shinned Hawk

2 distinctive facial stripes

long, rusty tail ♂

rusty wings and breast streaking

blue-gray crown with rusty cap

♀

♂

blue-gray wings

rusty barring on back

Nesting: in a tree cavity; may use a nest box; white to pale brown, spotted eggs are 1½ x 1⅛ in; mostly the female incubates 4–6 eggs for 29–30 days; both adults raise the young.

Did You Know?

No stranger to captivity, the American Kestrel was the first falcon to reproduce by artificial insemination.

Look For

An American Kestrel repeatedly lifts its tail while perched as it scouts below for prey.

American Coot
Fulica americana

This bird's behavior during the breeding season confirms the expression "crazy as a coot." It is aggressively territorial and constantly squabbles with other waterbirds in its space. You might catch a glimpse of an American Coot rushing across the water, flailing its wings and splashing an opponent. • With feet that have individually webbed toes, the coot is adapted to diving, but it isn't afraid to pilfer a meal from another skilled diver when a succulent piece of water celery is brought to the surface.

Other ID: red eyes; long, green-yellow legs; lobed toes.
Size: *L* 13–16 in; *W* 24 in.
Voice: calls frequently in summer, day and night: *kuk-kuk-kuk-kuk-kuk;* also croaks and grunts.
Status: common winter resident especially in the Coastal Plain and near the coast; occasional breeder in dense vegetation on the coast.
Habitat: shallow marshes, ponds and wetlands with open water and emergent vegetation; also sewage lagoons.

Similar Birds

Black Scoter

Pied-billed Grebe
(p. 36)

white, chickenlike bill with dark ring around tip

reddish spot on white forehead shield

white marks on tail

gray-black overall

Nesting: does not nest in Virginia; nests in north-central U.S. and Canada; in emergent vegetation; pair builds floating nest of cattails and grass; buffy white, brown-spotted eggs are 2 x 1⅜ in; pair incubates 8–12 eggs for 21–25 days.

Did You Know?

American Coots are the most widespread and abundant rails in North America.

Look For

Though it somewhat resembles a duck, an American Coot bobs its head while swimming or walking and has a narrower bill that extends up the forehead.

Killdeer

Charadrius vociferus

The Killdeer is a gifted actor, well known for its "broken wing" distraction display. When an intruder wanders too close to its nest, the Killdeer greets the interloper with piteous cries while dragging a wing and stumbling about as if injured. Most predators take the bait and pursue the bird. Once the Killdeer has lured the predator far away from its nest, it miraculously recovers from its "injury" and flies off with a loud call.

Other ID: brown head; white neck band; brown back and upperwings; white underparts; rufous rump. *Immature:* downy; only 1 breast band.
Size: *L* 9–11 in; W 24 in.
Voice: loud, distinctive *kill-dee kill-dee kill-deer;* variations include *deer-deer.*
Status: common permanent resident statewide; less common inland in winter.
Habitat: open areas, such as fields, lakeshores, sandy beaches, mudflats, gravel streambeds, wet meadows and grasslands.

Similar Birds

Semipalmated Plover

Piping Plover

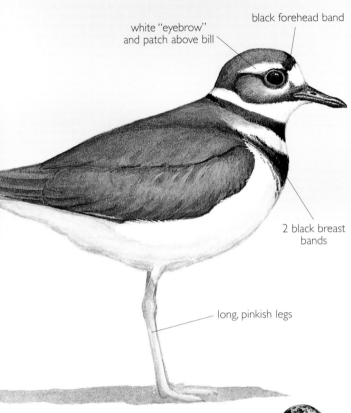

white "eyebrow" and patch above bill

black forehead band

2 black breast bands

long, pinkish legs

Nesting: on open ground; in a shallow, usually unlined depression; heavily marked, creamy buff eggs are 1⅜ x 1⅛ in; pair incubates 4 eggs for 24–28 days; may raise 2 broods.

Did You Know?

In spring, you might hear a European Starling imitate the vocal Killdeer's call.

Look For

The Killdeer has adapted well to urbanization, and it can be seen on golf courses, farms, in fields and abandoned industrial areas as often as on shorelines.

American Oystercatcher

Haematopus palliatus

One of the few birds with a bill sturdy enough to pry open a mollusk shell, the American Oystercatcher's diet includes oysters, clams and mussels. When its tastebuds cry out for more, it will gladly eat limpets, crabs, marine worms, sea urchins and even jellyfish. These large shorebirds usually forage alone and in silence, but issue loud whistles as they fly between mudflats and shellfish beds. • American Oystercatchers may form a breeding trio of two females and one male, tending up to two nests and taking care of the young for the first weeks.

Other ID: stocky build; short tail. *In flight:* bold, white wing stripe and rump patch.
Size: L 18½ in; W 32 in.
Voice: call is a loud *wheet*, often given in series during flight.
Status: common summer resident on barrier islands; less common in winter and in the Chesapeake.
Habitat: coastal marine habitats; will nest on dredge-spoil islands.

Look For

During the summer breeding season, watch for mating pairs performing their loud, piping courtship display.

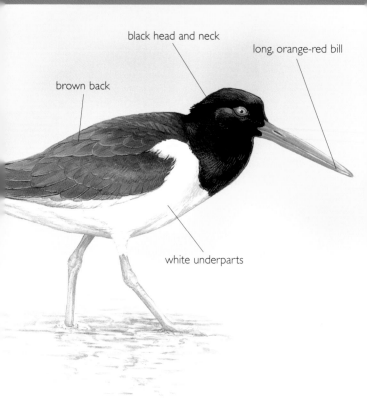

black head and neck

long, orange-red bill

brown back

white underparts

Nesting: scrape nest in a sandy depression may be lined with dead plants, shells or pebbles; boldly marked, yellowish to brown eggs are 2¼ x 1½ in; pair incubates 2–4 eggs for 24–27 days; may mate for life.

Did You Know?

When foraging, an oystercatcher will quickly stab its bill into an open mussel or oyster, severing the adductor muscle that holds the shells together. Then it can consume the soft inner parts. It also uses its bladelike bill tip to pry limpets off rocks.

Lesser Yellowlegs
Tringa flavipes

The "tattletale" Lesser Yellowlegs is the self-appointed sentinel in a mixed flock of shorebirds, raising the alarm at the first sign of a threat. • It is challenging to discern Lesser Yellowlegs and Greater Yellowlegs *(T. melanoleuca)* in the field, but with practice, you will notice that the Lesser's bill is finer, straighter and shorter, about as long as its head is wide. With long legs and wings, the Lesser appears slimmer and taller than the Greater, and it is more commonly seen in flocks. Finally, the Lesser Yellowlegs emits a pair of peeps, while the Greater Yellowlegs peeps three times.

Other ID: subtle, dark eye line; pale lores.
Nonbreeding: grayer overall.
Size: *L* 10–11 in; *W* 24 in.
Voice: typically a high-pitched pair of *tew* notes; noisiest on breeding grounds.
Status: common migrant at coast; less common inland; uncommon winter resident at coast.
Habitat: shorelines of lakes, rivers, marshes and ponds; coastal mudflats.

Similar Birds

Willet

Greater Yellowlegs

Solitary Sandpiper

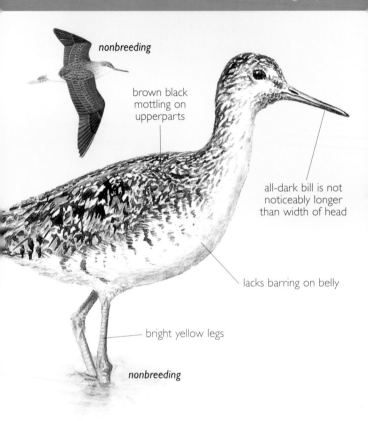

nonbreeding

brown black mottling on upperparts

all-dark bill is not noticeably longer than width of head

lacks barring on belly

bright yellow legs

nonbreeding

Nesting: does not nest in Virginia; nests in the Arctic; in open muskeg or a forest opening; in a depression on a dry mound lined with leaves and grass; darkly blotched, buff to olive eggs are 1⅝ x 1⅛ in; pair incubates 4 eggs for 22–23 days.

Did You Know?

Yellowlegs were popular game birds in the 1800s because they were plentiful and easy to shoot.

Look For

When feeding, the Lesser Yellowlegs wades into water almost to its belly, sweeping its bill back and forth just below the water's surface.

Sanderling
Calidris alba

The Sanderling is one of the world's most wide-spread shorebirds and graces sandy shorelines around the world. Running along the shore, the Sanderling chases the waves, snatching up aquatic invertebrates before they are swept back into the water. On shores where wave action is limited, it resorts to probing mudflats for a meal of mollusks and insects. • To keep warm, Sanderlings seek the company of roosting sandpipers or plovers and turnstones. They will also take a rest from their zigzag dance along a beach to stand with one leg tucked up, a posture that conserves body heat.

Other ID: *Nonbreeding:* pale gray upperparts; black shoulder patch (often concealed). *In flight:* dark leading edge of wing.
Size: *L* 7–8½ in; *W* 17 in.
Voice: flight call is a sharp *kip* or *plick*.
Status: common migrant and winter resident on the coast; uncommon in summer.
Habitat: sandy and muddy shorelines, spits.

Similar Birds

Baird's Sandpiper

Least Sandpiper

White-rumped Sandpiper

nonbreeding

broad, white
wing stripe

relatively short,
black bill

dark mottling on
rufous head, breast
and upperparts

white underparts

nonbreeding

Nesting: does not nest in Virginia; nests in the
Arctic; on the ground; cup nest is lined with leaves;
darkly blotched, olive eggs are 1½ x 1 in; both
sexes incubate 3–4 eggs for 23–24 days.

Did You Know?

The Sanderling breeds
throughout the Arctic
and winters on whatever
continent it chooses,
excluding Antarctica.

Look For

Sanderlings in pale nonbreeding plumage reflect a ghostly
glow as they forage at night
on moonlit beaches.

Laughing Gull

Larus atricilla

An incomplete white eye ring and drooping bill give black-headed Laughing Gulls a stately appearance. In keeping with their elegant look, these hooded gulls have taken up permanent residence along some of the best beachfront property on the Atlantic Coast. Still, they are not above begging for handouts and can be seen loitering in parking lots or following ferries. • Laughing Gulls were nearly extirpated from the Atlantic Coast in the late 19th century, when egg collecting was popular and feathers for women's hats were in high demand. East Coast populations have gradually recovered, and these gulls are once again common along Virginia's coastline.

Other ID: *Nonbreeding:* white head with some pale gray bands.
Size: L 15–17 in; W 3 ft.
Voice: loud, high-pitched, laughing call: *ha-ha-ha-ha-ha-ha.*
Status: common summer resident and migrant on the coast; less common in winter and during migration inland.
Habitat: primarily coastal in bays and estuaries; salt marshes and sandy beaches; occasionally inland shores, steams or landfills.

Similar Birds

Bonaparte's Gull

Little Gull

nonbreeding

black bill

black head

broken, white
eye ring

red bill

black legs

breeding

Nesting: colonial; on a dry island, sandy coastal beach or salt marsh; builds a cup nest of marsh vegetation on ground; brown-blotched, olive buff eggs are 2¼ x 1½ in; both parents incubate 3 eggs for 22–27 days.

Did You Know?

Nesting colonies on small offshore islands are vulnerable to spring storms and high tides that flood shoreline nests.

Look For

The Latin name *atricilla,* "black tail," refers to a black band present only on the tails of immature birds.

Ring-billed Gull

Larus delawarensis

Few people can claim that they have never seen this common and widespread gull. Highly tolerant of humans, Ring-billed Gulls are part of our everyday lives, scavenging our litter and fouling our parks. These omnivorous gulls will eat almost anything and swarm beaches, golf courses and fast-food restaurant parking lots looking for handouts, making pests of themselves. However, few species have adjusted to human development as well as the Ring-billed Gull, which is something to appreciate.

Other ID: yellow eyes. *Breeding:* white head. *In flight:* black wing tips with a few white spots.
Size: *L* 18–20 in; *W* 4 ft.
Voice: high-pitched *kakakaka-akakaka;* also a low, laughing *yook-yook-yook.*
Status: common winter resident and migrant statewide; more abundant on coast.
Habitat: *Breeding:* bare, rocky and shrubby islands and sewage ponds. *In migration* and *winter:* lakes, rivers, landfills, golf courses, fields and parks.

Similar Birds

Herring Gull

Glaucous Gull

nonbreeding

brownish streaks on head and neck

black ring around tip of yellow bill

pale gray mantle

nonbreeding

yellow legs

white underparts

Nesting: does not nest in Virginia; nests in northern U.S. and Canada; colonial; scrape nest on the ground is lined with grass and small sticks; brown-blotched, gray to olive eggs are 2⅜ x 1⅝ in; pair incubates 2–4 eggs for 23–28 days.

Did You Know?

In chaotic nesting colonies, adult Ring-billed Gulls will call out for their young and can recognize the response of their chicks.

Look For

To differentiate between gulls, pay attention to the markings on their bills and the color of their legs and eyes.

Great Black-backed Gull

Larus marinus

The Great Black-backed Gull's commanding size and slate black mantle set it apart from other seabirds, but only adults have this distinctive plumage. For the first four years, immature gulls have dark streaking or mottling, which camouflages them from predators. • Like many marine gulls, the Great Black-backed can drink salt water. Excess salt is removed from its bloodstream by tiny, specialized glands located above the eyes. The salty fluid then dribbles out of the bird's nostrils.

Other ID: *Nonbreeding:* may have faintly streaked nape. *In flight:* gray on trailing edge of underwing; white spots on wing tips.
Size: *L* 30 in; *W* 5½ ft.
Voice: a harsh *kyow.*
Status: common permanent resident at the coast.
Habitat: harbors, bays, landfills and open water on large lakes and rivers.

Similar Birds

Glaucous Gull

Lesser Black-backed Gull

slate black mantle

yellow bill with
red spot

pale pinkish legs

breeding

Nesting: nests sparingly on barrier and
Chesapeake Bay islands; usually colonial; on an
island, cliff top or beach; on the ground in a
mound of vegetation and debris; brown-blotched,
olive to buff eggs are 3 x 2⅛ in; pair incubates
2–3 eggs for 27–28 days.

Did You Know?

These opportunistic
feeders eat fish, eggs, invertebrates and small mam-
mals. They may also pirate
food from other birds or
scavenge at landfills.

Look For

A threatened gull will point
its bill down, stretch out its
neck and walk stiffly to warn
away intruders.

Royal Tern

Sterna maxima

Female Royal Terns lay a single egg (sometimes two) amid a tightly packed colony of up to 10,000 nests. Both adults take responsibility for incubating their treasure through hot, sun-drenched days and cool coastal nights. Most of the eggs in the colony hatch within a period of a few days, turning the beach colony into a raucous muddle of commotion. Parenting terns order the chaos by shepherding their semi-precocial young into a massive herd of fluffy, hungry newborns known as a "creche." Constantly supervised by incoming squadrons of food-carrying adults, young in the creche remain well protected.

Other ID: narrow, dark edging on outer underwing primaries; white underparts; pale gray upperparts. *Nonbreeding:* loses black cap but maintains frayed black fringe at back of head.
Size: *L* 20 in; *W* 3½ ft.
Voice: bleating call is a high-pitched *kee-er*; also gives a whistling *turreee*.
Status: common coastal migrant and summer resident; uncommon to rare in winter.
Habitat: coastal habitats including sandy beaches, estuaries and saltwater marshes.

Similar Birds

Forster's Tern   Common Tern   Black Skimmer   Sandwich Tern

deeply forked tail

black cap is frayed
at back of head

long, orange bill

thick, dark wedge on
tips of upperwing

legs usually black

breeding

Nesting: colonial; usually on sandy ground; nest is
a shallow depression lined sparsely with vegetation;
heavily marked, ivory eggs are 2½ x 1¾ in; pair
incubates 1–2 eggs for 20–25 days.

Did You Know?

Adults returning to tightly
packed nesting colonies
can recognize their own
young by voice.

Look For

During breeding season, the
male Royal Tern performs
spiraling aerial flights, then
struts in front of the female
with offerings of fish.

Rock Pigeon
Columba livia

The colorful and familiar Rock Pigeons have an unusual feature: they feed their young a substance similar to milk. These birds lack mammary glands, but they produce a nutritious liquid, called "pigeon milk," in their crops. A chick inserts its bills down the adult's throat to reach the thick, protein-rich fluid. • This pigeon is likely a descendant of a Eurasian bird that was first domesticated about 4500 BC. The Rock Pigeon was introduced to North America in the 17th century by European colonists.

Other ID: *In flight:* holds wings in a deep "V" when gliding.
Size: *L* 12–13 in; *W* 28 in (male is usually larger).
Voice: soft, cooing *coorrr-coorrr-coorrr*.
Status: common permanent resident statewide.
Habitat: urban areas, railroad yards and agricultural areas; high cliffs provide more natural habitat for some.

Similar Birds

Mourning Dove

Look For

No other "wild" bird varies as much in coloration, a result of semi-domestication and extensive inbreeding over time.

color is highly variable
(iridescent blue-gray,
red, white or tan)

usually has
white rump

orange feet

Nesting: in a barn or on a cliff, bridge or tower; in a flimsy nest of sticks, grass and other vegetation; glossy white eggs are 1½ x 1⅛ in; pair incubates 2 eggs for 16–19 days; may raise broods year-round.

Did You Know?

Much of our understanding of bird migration, endocrinology, color genetics and sensory perception comes from experiments involving Rock Pigeons, the most studied birds in the world.

Mourning Dove

Zenaida macroura

The Mourning Dove's soft cooing, which filters through broken woodlands and suburban parks, is often confused with the sound of a hooting owl. Curious birders who track down the source of the calls are often surprised to find the streamlined silhouette of a perched dove. • This popular game animal is one of the most abundant native birds in North America. Its numbers and range have increased because human development has created more open habitats and food sources, such as waste grain and bird feeders.

Other ID: buffy, gray-brown plumage; small head; dark bill; sleek body; dull red legs.
Size: *L* 11–13 in; *W* 18 in.
Voice: mournful, soft, slow *oh-woe-woe-woe*.
Status: common permanent resident statewide.
Habitat: open and riparian woodlands, forest edges, agricultural and suburban areas, open parks.

Similar Birds

Rock Pigeon
(p. 80)

Black-billed Cuckoo

Yellow-billed Cuckoo
(p. 84)

pale blue eye ring

dark, shiny patch
below ear

black spots on
upperwing

pale rosy
underparts

long, white-trimmed,
tapering tail

Nesting: in a shrub or tree; occasionally on the ground; nest is a fragile, shallow platform of twigs; white eggs are 1⅛ x ⅞ in; pair incubates 2 eggs for 14 days.

Did You Know?

The Mourning Dove raises up to six broods each year—more than any other native bird.

Look For

When the Mourning Dove bursts into flight, its wings clap above and below its body. You may also hear a whistling sound as this bird flies at high speed.

Yellow-billed Cuckoo
Coccyzus americanus

Large tracts of hardwood forest, such as Pocahontas State Forest, provide valuable habitat for the Yellow-billed Cuckoo, a bird that is declining over much of its range and has already disappeared in some states. Songbirds are increasingly vulnerable to predators in the patchy, fragmented forests left behind by human development. The cuckoo's habitat has also deteriorated over the years as waterways have been altered or dammed. • Most of the time, the Yellow-billed Cuckoo lives silently within impenetrable, deciduous undergrowth, relying on obscurity for survival. Then, for a short period during nesting, the male cuckoo tempts fate by issuing a barrage of loud, rhythmic courtship calls.

Other ID: olive brown upperparts; white underparts.
Size: *L* 11–13 in; *W* 18 in.
Voice: long series of deep, hollow *kuks,* slowing near the end: *kuk-kuk-kuk-kuk kuk kop kow kowlp kowlp.*
Status: common to uncommon summer resident statewide.
Habitat: semi-open deciduous habitats; dense tangles and thickets at orchard edges, urban parks, farm fields, roadways; sometimes woodlots.

Similar Birds

Black-billed Cuckoo

Mourning Dove
(p. 82)

yellow eye ring

rufous tinge on
primaries

mainly yellow, downcurved
bill with black upper
mandible ridge

long tail with large, white
spots on underside

Nesting: on a low horizontal branch in a deciduous shrub or small tree; flimsy platform nest of
twigs is lined with grass; pale bluish green eggs are
1¼ x ⅞ in; pair incubates 3–4 eggs for 9–11 days.

Did You Know?

The Yellow-billed Cuckoo
or "Rain Crow" has a
propensity for calling on
dark, cloudy days and a
reputation for predicting
rainstorms.

Look For

Yellow-billed Cuckoos breed
in higher densities and lay
larger clutches when out-
breaks of cicadas or tent
caterpillars provide an
abundant food supply.

Eastern Screech-Owl
Megascops asio

red morph

The diminutive Eastern Screech-Owl is a year-round resident of low-elevation, deciduous woodlands, but its presence is rarely detected. Most screech-owls sleep away the daylight hours snuggled safely inside tree cavities, artificial nest boxes or conifers, especially small red-cedars. • Adaptable screech-owls have one of the most varied diets of any owl, capturing small animals, earthworms, insects and sometimes even snagging fish from creeks. • Unique among the owls found in our region, Eastern Screech-Owls show both red and gray color morphs. In Virginia, the gray morph is more common. Very rarely, an intermediate brown morph occurs.

Other ID: reddish or grayish overall; yellow eyes.
Size: *L* 8–9 in; *W* 20–22 in.
Voice: horselike "whinny" that rises and falls.
Status: common permanent resident statewide.
Habitat: mature deciduous forests, open deciduous and riparian woodlands, orchards and shade trees with natural cavities.

Similar Birds

Northern Saw-whet Owl

Long-eared Owl

Great Horned Owl
(p. 88)

short "ear" tufts

pale grayish bill

dark breast streaking

gray morph

Nesting: in a natural cavity or artificial nest box; no lining is added; white eggs are 1½ x 1⅜ in; female incubates 4–5 eggs for about 26 days; male brings food to the female during incubation.

Did You Know?

Eastern Screech-Owls respond readily to whistled imitations of their calls, and sometimes several owls appear to investigate the fraudulent perpetrator.

Look For

Mobbing chickadees or squawking Blue Jays can alert you to an owl's presence. They may mob a screech-owl after losing a family member during the night.

Great Horned Owl
Bubo virginianus

This highly adaptable and superbly camouflaged hunter has sharp hearing and powerful vision that allow it to hunt at night as well as by day. It will swoop down from a perch onto almost any small creature that moves. • An owl has specially designed feathers on its wings to reduce noise. The leading edges of the flight feathers are fringed rather than smooth, which interrupts airflow over the wing and allows the owl to fly noiselessly. • Great Horned Owls begin their courtship as early as January, and by February and March, the females are already incubating their eggs.

Other ID: overall plumage varies from light gray to dark brown; heavily mottled, gray, brown and black upperparts; yellow eyes; white "chin."
Size: *L* 18–25 in; *W* 3–5 ft.
Voice: breeding call is 4–6 deep hoots: *hoo-hoo-hoooo hoo-hoo* or *Who's awake? Me too;* female gives higher-pitched hoots.
Status: common permanent resident statewide.
Habitat: fragmented forests, fields, riparian woodlands, suburban parks and wooded edges of landfills.

Similar Birds

Long-eared Owl

Eastern Screech-Owl
(p. 86)

tall, widely spaced "ear" tufts form a triangle with beak

rusty orange facial disc is outlined in black

fine, horizontal barring on breast

Nesting: in another bird's abandoned stick nest or in a tree cavity; adds little or no nest material; dull whitish eggs are $2\frac{1}{4}$ x $1\frac{7}{8}$ in; mostly the female incubates 2–3 eggs for 28–35 days.

Did You Know?

The Great Horned Owl has a poor sense of smell, which might explain why it is the only consistent predator of skunks.

Look For

Owls regurgitate pellets that contain the indigestible parts of their prey. You can find these pellets, which are generally clean and dry, under frequently used perches.

Barred Owl
Strix varia

The adaptable Barred Owl is found in many woodland habitats throughout Virginia, especially those near water. It uses large tracts of mature forest, ranging from swampy bottomlands to higher, mixedwood forests in the Appalachian Mountains. • Each spring, the escalating laughs, hoots and gargling howls of Barred Owls reinforce pair bonds. These birds tend to be more vocal during late evening and early morning when the moon is full, the air is calm and the sky is clear.

Other ID: mottled, dark gray-brown plumage.
Size: L 17–24 in; W 3½–4 ft.
Voice: loud, hooting, rhythmic, laughing call is heard mostly in spring: *Who cooks for you? Who cooks for you all?*
Status: common permanent resident statewide.
Habitat: mature coniferous and mixed forests, especially in dense stands near swamps, streams and lakes.

Similar Birds

Great Horned Owl
(p. 88)

Short-eared Owl

no "ear" tufts

dark eyes

pale bill

horizontal barring
around neck and
upper breast

vertical streaking
on belly

Nesting: in a natural tree cavity, broken treetop
or abandoned stick nest; adds very little material
to the nest; white eggs are 2 x 1⅝ in; female
incubates 2–3 eggs for 28–33 days.

Did You Know?

In darkness, the Barred
Owl's eyesight may be 100
times keener than that of
humans, and it is able to
locate and follow prey
using sound alone.

Look For

Dark eyes make the Barred
Owl unique—most familiar
large owls in North America
have yellow eyes.

Whip-poor-will

Caprimulgus vociferus

These magical, elusive birds blend seamlessly into lichen-covered bark or the forest floor. On spring evenings, their airy, soothing *whip-poor-will* calls float through the open woodlands, signaling that breeding season has begun. Whip-poor-wills are thought to time their egg laying to the lunar cycle so that hatchlings can be fed more efficiently during the light of the full moon. • The Whip-poor-will is a member of the nightjar or "goatsucker" family, so named during the days of Aristotle, when superstition held that these birds would suck milk from the udders of female goats, causing the goats to go blind.

Other ID: mottled, brown-gray overall with black flecking; large eyes; relatively long, rounded tail. *Red morph:* mottled, rufous overall; pale gray markings on wings.
Size: *L* 9–10 in; *W* 16–20 in.
Voice: whistled *whip-poor-will,* with emphasis on the *will.*
Status: locally common summer resident statewide; less common in the Coastal Plain and at higher elevations.
Habitat: open deciduous and pine woodlands; often along forest edges.

Similar Birds

Chuck-will's-widow

Common Nighthawk

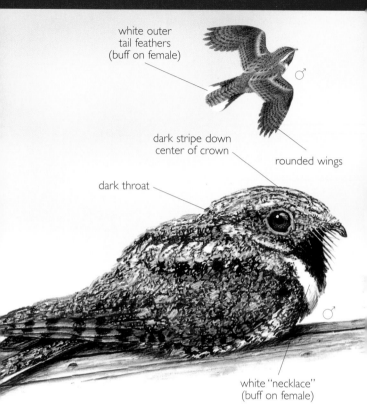

white outer
tail feathers
(buff on female)

♂

dark stripe down
center of crown

rounded wings

dark throat

♂

white "necklace"
(buff on female)

Nesting: on the ground in leaf or pine needle litter; no nest is built; brown-blotched, whitish eggs are 1¼ x ⅞ in; female incubates 2 eggs for 19–20 days; both adults raise the young.

Did You Know?

Within days of hatching, young Whip-poor-wills can scurry away from their nest in search of protective cover if disturbed.

Look For

Cryptic plumage, sleepy daytime habits and secretive nesting behavior mean a hopeful observer must literally stumble upon a Whip-poor-will to see one.

Chimney Swift
Chaetura pelagica

Chimney Swifts are the "frequent fliers" of the bird world—they feed, drink, bathe, collect nesting material and even mate while they fly! Much of their time is spent sailing above our urban neighborhoods in search of insects. • In fall, large flocks of migrating swifts assemble at large chimneys to roost. Chimney Swifts have small, weak legs and cannot take flight again if they land on the ground. For this reason, swifts usually cling to vertical surfaces with their strong claws.

Other ID: brown overall; slim body. *In flight:* rapid wingbeats; erratic flight pattern.
Size: L 5–5½ in; W 12–13 in.
Voice: call is a rapid *chitter-chitter-chitter,* given in flight; also gives a rapid series of staccato *chip* notes.
Status: common summer resident and migrant statewide.
Habitat: forages above cities and towns; roosts and nests in chimneys; may nest in tree cavities in more remote areas.

Similar Birds

Northern Rough-
winged Swallow

Bank Swallow

Cliff Swallow

boomerang-shaped
profile in flight

long, thin, pointed,
crescent-shaped wings

squared tail

Nesting: often colonial; half-saucer nest of short, dead twigs is attached to a vertical wall; white eggs are ¾ x ½ in; pair incubates 4–5 eggs for 19–21 days.

Did You Know?

Migrating Chimney Swifts may fly as high as 10,000 feet; above this altitude aircraft are required to carry oxygen.

Look For

Swifts frequently nest in brick chimneys or abandoned buildings and use saliva to attach their half-saucer nests to the walls.

Ruby-throated Hummingbird

Archilochus colubris

Ruby-throated Hummingbirds bridge the ecological gap between birds and bees—they feed on sweet, energy-rich flower nectar and pollinate flowers in the process. You can attract hummingbirds to your backyard with a sugarwater feeder filled with one part sugar to four parts water (red food coloring is harmful to hummingbirds) or with native nectar-producing flowers such as honeysuckle. • Each year, Ruby-throated Hummingbirds migrate across the Gulf of Mexico—a nonstop, 500-mile journey.

Other ID: thin, needlelike bill; pale underparts.
Size: *L* 3½–4 in; *W* 4–4½ in.
Voice: a loud *chick* and other high squeaks; soft buzzing of the wings while in flight.
Status: common summer resident and migrant statewide.
Habitat: open, mixed woodlands, wetlands, orchards, tree-lined meadows, flower gardens and backyards with trees and feeders.

Similar Birds

Rufous Hummingbird

Look For

Hummingbirds are among the few birds that can fly vertically and in reverse.

fine, dark streaking on white throat

♀

iridescent, green back

♂

black "chin" with ruby red throat on male

dark tail

Nesting: on a horizontal tree limb; tiny, deep cup nest of plant down and fibers is held together with spider silk; lichens and leaves are pasted on the exterior walls; white eggs are ½ x ⅜ in; female incubates 2 eggs for 13–16 days.

Did You Know?

In straight-ahead flight, hummingbirds beat their wings up to 80 times per second, and their hearts can beat up to 1200 times per minute! Weighing about as much as a nickel, a hummingbird can briefly reach speeds of up to 60 miles per hour.

Belted Kingfisher
Ceryle alcyon

Perched on a bare branch over a productive pool, the Belted Kingfisher utters a scratchy, rattling call. Then, with little regard for its scruffy hairdo, it plunges headfirst into the water and snags a fish or frog. Back on its perch, the kingfisher flips its prey into the air and swallows it headfirst. Similar to owls, kingfishers regurgitate the indigestible portion of their food as pellets. • Nestlings have closed eyes and are featherless for the first week. Their first food is partially digested fish regurgitated by the adults, but after five days they can swallow small fingerling fish whole.

Other ID: bluish upperparts; long, small, white patch near eye; straight bill; short legs; white underwings.
Size: *L* 11–14 in; *W* 20–21 in.
Voice: fast, repetitive, cackling rattle, like a teacup shaking on a saucer.
Status: common permanent resident statewide; less common in mountains in winter.
Habitat: rivers, large streams, lakes, marshes and beaver ponds, especially near exposed soil banks, gravel pits or bluffs.

Similar Birds

Blue Jay (p. 118)

Look For

The Belted Kingfisher often flies very close to the water, so close, in fact, that its wing tips may skim the surface.

shaggy crest

white "collar"

♀

rust-colored "belt"
on female may be
incomplete

♂

blue-gray
breast band

Nesting: in a cavity at the end of an earth
burrow; glossy white eggs are 1⅜ x 1 in; pair
incubates 6–7 eggs for 22–24 days.

Did You Know?

Kingfisher pairs nest on sandy banks near water and
use their sturdy bills and claws to dig burrows that may
measure up to 6 feet long.

Red-bellied Woodpecker

Melanerpes carolinus

Red-bellied Woodpeckers are no strangers to sub-urban backyards and will sometimes nest in bird-houses. This widespread bird is found year-round in woodlands throughout the eastern states, but its numbers fluctuate depending on habitat availability and weather conditions. • These birds often issue noisy, rolling *churr* calls as they poke around wooded landscapes in search of seeds, fruit and a variety of insects. Unlike most woodpeckers, Red-bellies consume large amounts of plant material, seldom excavating wood for insects.

Other ID: reddish tinge on belly. *Juvenile:* dark gray crown; streaked breast.
Size: *L* 9–10½ in; *W* 16 in.
Voice: call is a soft, rolling *churr*; drums in second-long bursts.
Status: common permanent resident statewide.
Habitat: mature deciduous woodlands; occasionally in wooded residential areas.

Similar Birds

Northern Flicker
(p. 104)

Red-headed Woodpecker

black and white barring on back ♂

red nape extends to forehead

red on nape only ♀

white patches on rump and topside base of primaries

Nesting: in a woodland or residential area; in a cavity excavated by mainly by the male; white eggs are 1 x ¾ in; pair incubates 4–5 eggs for 12–14 days.

Did You Know?

Studies of banded Red-bellied Woodpeckers have shown that these birds have a life span in the wild of more than 20 years.

Look For

The Red-bellied Woodpecker's namesake is only a small reddish area that is difficult to see in the field.

Hairy Woodpecker

Picoides villosus

Catching a glimpse of a Hairy Woodpecker at your backyard feeder is a treat, because they tend to visit less frequently than the similar Downy Woodpecker (*P. pubescens*). At close range, the Hairy's all-white outer tail feathers and larger size become more apparent. These birds are quite aggressive at feeders, often thrashing seeds around with their sturdy bills.
• Most woodpeckers have a very long tongue—sometimes more than four times the length of the bill—that is wrapped around the skull similar to the way a measuring tape is stored in its case. The tip of the long, maneuverable tongue is sticky with saliva and is finely barbed to help seize wood-boring insects.

ID: black wings, usually with fewer white markings than the Downy; pure white belly. *Female:* no red patch on head.
Size: *L* 8–9½ in; *W* 15 in.
Voice: loud, sharp call: *peek peek;* long, unbroken trill: *keek-ik-ik-ik-ik-ik;* drums less regularly and at a lower pitch than the Downy.
Status: fairly common permanent resident statewide; less common in the Coastal Plain.
Habitat: lowland deciduous and mixed forests; burned areas.

Similar Birds

Downy Woodpecker

Yellow-bellied
Sapsucker

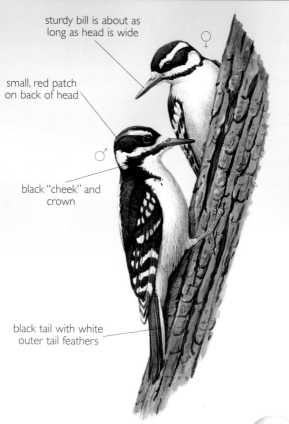

sturdy bill is about as long as head is wide

♀

small, red patch on back of head

♂

black "cheek" and crown

black tail with white outer tail feathers

Nesting: pair excavates a nest site in a live or decaying tree trunk or limb; cavity is lined with wood chips; white eggs are 1 x ¾ in; pair incubates 4–5 eggs for 12–14 days; both adults feed the young.

Did You Know?

Woodpeckers have feathered nostrils, which filter out the sawdust produced by hammering.

Look For

Both Hairy and Downy Woodpeckers have white outer tail feathers, but the Hairy's are pure white, while the Downy's have several dark spots.

Northern Flicker
Colaptes auratus

Instead of boring holes in trees, the Northern
Flicker scours the ground in search of invertebrates,
particularly ants. With robinlike hops, it investigates
anthills, grassy meadows and forest clearings.
• Flickers often bathe in dusty depressions. The dust
particles absorb oils and bacteria that can harm the
birds' feathers. To clean themselves even more
thoroughly, flickers squash captured ants and
preen themselves with the remains. Ants
contain formic acid, which kills small parasites on the flickers' skin and feathers.

Other ID: long bill; brownish to buff face; gray crown;
white rump. *Male:* black "mustache" stripe. *Female:* no
"mustache."
Size: *L* 12–13 in; *W* 20 in.
Voice: loud, "laughing," rapid *kick-kick-kick-kick-kick-kick;
woika-woika-woika* issued during courtship.
Status: common permanent resident statewide; more
common in migration.
Habitat: *Breeding:* open woodlands and forest edges,
fields, meadows, beaver ponds and other wetlands.
In migration and *winter:* coastal vegetation,
offshore islands, urban gardens.

Similar Birds

Red-bellied
Woodpecker (p. 100)

Yellow-bellied
Sapsucker

black barring on
brown back and wings

black-spotted, buff to
whitish underparts

♂

red nape
crescent

black "bib"

♀

yellow underwings
and undertail

"Yellow-shafted Flicker"

Nesting: pair excavates a cavity in a dying or
decaying trunk and lines it with wood chips; may
also use a nest box; white eggs are 1⅛ x ⅞ in;
pair incubates 5–8 eggs for 11–16 days.

Did You Know?

Most woodpeckers have
zygodactyl feet: each foot
has two toes facing forward
and two toes facing back,
which helps the bird move
up and down tree trunks.

Look For

Northern Flickers prefer to
forage at anthills and may
visit their favorite colonies
regularly, hammering and
probing into the ground to
unearth adults and larvae.

Pileated Woodpecker
Dryocopus pileatus

The Pileated Woodpecker, with its flaming red crest, chisel-like bill and commanding size, requires 100 acres of mature forest as a home territory. In Virginia, the patchwork of woodlots and small towns limits the availability of continuous habitat, requiring this woodpecker to show itself more. • A pair will spend up to six weeks excavating a large nest cavity in a dead or decaying tree. Ducks, small falcons, owls and even flying squirrels frequently nest in abandoned Pileated Woodpecker cavities.

Other ID: predominantly black; yellow eyes; white "chin." *Male:* red "mustache." *Female:* no red "mustache"; gray-brown forehead.
Size: L 16–17 in; W 28–29 in.
Voice: loud, fast, rolling *woika-woika-woika-woika;* long series of *kuk* notes; loud, resonant drumming.
Status: fairly common to common permanent resident statewide.
Habitat: extensive tracts of mature forests; riparian woodlands or woodlots in suburban and agricultural areas.

Similar Birds

Yellow-bellied
Sapsucker

Red-headed
Woodpecker

Red-bellied
Woodpecker (p. 100)

flaming red crest extends farther on male

stout, dark bill

♂

white stripe runs from bill to shoulder

♀

white wing linings

Nesting: pair excavates a cavity in a dead or decaying trunk and lines it with wood chips; white eggs are 1¼ x 1 in; pair incubates 4 eggs for 15–18 days.

Did You Know?

A woodpecker's bill becomes shorter as the bird ages, so juvenile birds have slightly longer bills than adults.

Look For

Foraging Pileated Woodpeckers leave large, rectangular cavities up to 12 inches long near the base of trees.

Eastern Phoebe
Sayornis phoebe

Whether you are poking around a barnyard, campground picnic shelter or your backyard shed, there is a very good chance you will stumble upon an Eastern Phoebe family and its marvelous mud nest. The Eastern Phoebe's nest building and territorial defense is normally well underway by the time most other songbirds arrive in Virginia in mid-May. Once limited to nesting on natural cliffs and fallen riparian trees, this adaptive flycatcher has gradually found success nesting in culverts and under bridges and eaves, especially when water is near.

Other ID: white underparts with gray wash on breast and sides; no eye ring; no obvious wing bars; dark legs.
Size: L 6½–7 in; W 10½ in.
Voice: *Male:* song is a hearty, snappy *fee-bee, delivered* frequently; call is a sharp *chip.*
Status: common summer resident and migrant statewide; becoming uncommon in winter.
Habitat: open deciduous woodlands, forest edges and clearings; usually near water.

Similar Birds

Eastern Wood-Pewee

Acadian Flycatcher

Eastern Kingbird
(p. 112)

dark head and bill

gray-brown
upperparts

belly may be
washed with
yellow in fall

breeding

frequently pumps its tail

Nesting: under the ledge of a building, picnic shelter or bridge, on a cliff, or in a culvert or well; cup-shaped mud nest is lined with soft material; unmarked, white eggs are ¾ x ⁹⁄₁₆ in; female incubates 4–5 eggs for about 16 days.

Did You Know?

Eastern Phoebes sometimes reuse their nest sites for many years. A female that saves energy by reusing her nest is often able to lay more eggs.

Look For

Some other birds pump their tails while perched, but few species can match the zest and frequency of the Eastern Phoebe's tail pumping.

Great Crested Flycatcher

Myiarchus crinitus

Loud, raucous calls give away the presence of the brightly colored Great Crested Flycatcher. This large flycatcher often inhabits forest edges and nests in woodlands throughout our region. Unlike other eastern flycatchers, the Great Crested prefers to nest in a natural tree cavity or abandoned woodpecker hole, or sometimes uses a nest box intended for a bluebird. • The Great Crested Flycatcher often decorates its nest entrance with a shed snakeskin or substitutes translucent plastic wrap. The purpose of this practice is not fully understood, though it might make any would-be predators think twice.

Other ID: dark olive brown upperparts; heavy, black bill.
Size: *L* 8–9 in; *W* 13 in.
Voice: loud, whistled *wheep!* and a rolling *prrrrreet!*
Status: common summer resident statewide.
Habitat: deciduous and mixed woodlands and forests, usually near openings or edges.

Similar Birds

Acadian Flycatcher

Eastern Kingbird
(p. 112)

peaked, crested head

gray throat and upper breast

bright yellow belly and undertail coverts

reddish brown tail

Nesting: in a tree cavity or artificial cavity lined with grasses; may hang a shed snakeskin over entrance hole; heavily marked, creamy white to pale buff eggs are $7/8$ x $5/8$ in; female incubates 5 eggs for 13–15 days.

Did You Know?

Many animals depend on tree cavities for shelter and nesting, so instead of cutting down large, dead trees, consider leaving a few standing.

Look For

Follow the loud *wheep!* calls and watch for a show of bright yellow and rufous feathers to find this flycatcher.

Eastern Kingbird
Tyrannus tyrannus

The Eastern Kingbird is sometimes referred to as the "Jekyll and Hyde" bird because it is a gregarious fruit eater while wintering in South America and an antisocial, aggressive insect eater while nesting in North America. The Eastern Kingbird fearlessly attacks crows, hawks and even humans that pass through its territory, pursuing and pecking at them until it feels the threat has passed. No one familiar with its pugnacious behavior will refute its scientific name, *Tyrannus tyrannus*. The Eastern Kingbird reveals a gentler side of its character in its quivering, butterfly-like courtship flight.

Other ID: black bill; no eye ring; white underparts; black legs.
Size: *L* 8½–9 in; *W* 15 in.
Voice: call is a quick, loud, chattering *kit-kit-kitter-kitter;* also a *buzzy dzee-dzee-dzee.*
Status: common summer resident statewide; very common on coast in migration.
Habitat: fields with scattered shrubs, trees or hedgerows, forest fringes, clearings, shrubby roadsides, towns and farmyards.

Similar Birds

Acadian Flycatcher

Eastern Wood-Pewee

Least Flycatcher

thin, orange-red crown
(rarely seen)

small head
crest

dark gray to black
upperparts

white-tipped tail

Nesting: on a horizontal tree limb, stump or upturned tree root; cup nest is made of weeds, twigs and grass; darkly blotched, white to pinkish eggs are 1 x ¾ in; female incubates 3–4 eggs for 14–18 days.

Did You Know?

Eastern Kingbirds rarely walk or hop on the ground—they prefer to fly, even for very short distances.

Look For

Eastern Kingbirds are common and widespread. On a drive in the country you will likely spot at least one of these birds sitting on a fence or utility wire.

Loggerhead Shrike
Lanius ludovicianus

The Loggerhead Shrike resembles a Northern Mockingbird and has the hunting habits of a hawk, putting it in a class of its own. This predatory songbird has very acute vision, and it often perches atop trees and on wires to scan for small prey, which is caught in fast, direct flight or a swooping dive. • Males display their hunting prowess by impaling prey on thorns or barbed wire. This behavior may also serve as a means of storing excess food during times of plenty. • Many shrikes become traffic fatalities when they fly low across roads to prey on insects attracted to the warm pavement.

Other ID: gray crown and back; white underparts. *In flight:* white wing patches.
Size: *L* 9 in; *W* 12 in.
Voice: *Male:* high-pitched, hiccupy *bird-ee bird*-ee in summer; infrequently a harsh *shack-shack* year-round.
Status: threatened; uncommon to rare permanent resident in the Shenandoah and southern Piedmont.
Habitat: grazed pastures and marginal and abandoned farmlands with scattered hawthorn shrubs, fence posts, barbed wire and nearby wetlands.

Similar Birds

Northern Mockingbird
(p. 142)

Look For

Shrikes typically perch at the top of tall trees to survey the surrounding area for prey.

thick, hooked bill

black "mask" extends
above hooked bill
onto forehead

black wings

whitish throat
patch

black tail with
white edges

Nesting: low in a shrub or small tree; bulky cup nest of twigs and grass is lined with animal hair, feathers and plant down; darkly spotted, pale eggs are 1 x ¾ in; female incubates 5–6 eggs for 15–17 days.

Did You Know?

Habitat loss has contributed to a steady decline in Loggerhead Shrike populations, earning this bird endangered species status in some regions of North America. Of the world's 30 shrike species, the Loggerhead is the only one that occurs exclusively in North America.

Red-eyed Vireo
Vireo olivaceus

Capable of delivering about 40 phrases per minute, the male Red-eyed Vireo can out-sing any one of his courting neighbors. One tenacious male set a record by singing 21,000 phrases in one day! Though you may still hear the Red-eyed Vireo singing five or six hours after other songbirds have ceased for the day, this bird is not easy to spot. With its olive brown plumage, it is well concealed among the foliage of deciduous trees. Its unique red eyes, unusual among songbirds, are even trickier to spot without a good pair of binoculars.

Other ID: black-bordered, olive "cheek"; olive green upperparts; white to pale gray underparts.
Size: L 6 in; W 10 in.
Voice: call is a short, scolding *rreeah*. *Male:* song is a series of quick, continuous, variable phrases with pauses in between: *look-up, way-up, tree-top, see-me, here-I-am!*
Status: common summer resident and migrant statewide.
Habitat: deciduous or mixed wood-lands with a shrubby understory.

Similar Birds

White-eyed Vireo

Philadelphia Vireo

Warbling Vireo

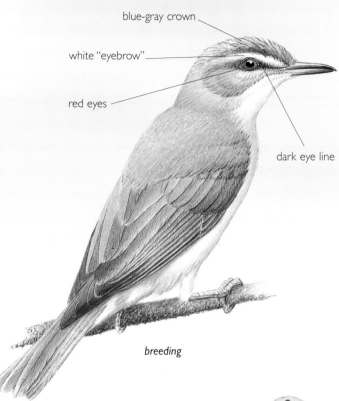

blue-gray crown

white "eyebrow"

red eyes

dark eye line

breeding

Nesting: in a tree or shrub; hanging cup nest is made of grass, roots, spider silk and cocoons; darkly spotted, white eggs are ¾ x ½ in; female incubates 4 eggs for 11–14 days.

Did You Know?

If its nest is parasitized by a Brown-headed Cowbird, the Red-eyed Vireo will respond by abandoning the eggs or by raising the cowbird young with its own.

Look For

The Red-eyed Vireo perches with a hunched stance and hops with its body turned diagonally to its direction of travel.

Blue Jay

Cyanocitta cristata

In our region, the Blue Jay is the only member of the corvid family dressed in blue. White-flecked wing feathers and sharply defined facial features make the Blue Jay easy to recognize. • Jays can be quite aggressive when competing for sunflower seeds and peanuts at backyard feeding stations and rarely hesitate to drive away smaller birds, squirrels or even threatening cats. Even the Great Horned Owl is not too formidable a predator for a group of these brave, boisterous mobsters to harass.

Other ID: blue upperparts; white underparts; black bill.
Size: *L* 11–12 in; *W* 16 in.
Voice: noisy, screaming *jay-jay-jay;* nasal *queedle queedle queedle-queedle* sounds like a muted trumpet; often imitates various sounds, including calls of other birds.
Status: common permanent resident statewide with large numbers of migrants passing through.
Habitat: mixed deciduous forests, agricultural areas, scrubby fields and townsites.

Similar Birds

Belted Kingfisher
(p. 98)

Eastern Bluebird
(p. 134)

blue crest

black "necklace"

white bar and flecking
on wings

dark bars and white
corners on blue tail

Nesting: in a tree or tall shrub; pair builds a
bulky stick nest; greenish, buff or pale eggs, spotted with gray and brown, are 1⅛ x ¾ in; pair
incubates 4–5 eggs for 16–18 days.

Did You Know?

Blue Jays store food from
feeders in trees and other
places for later use.

Look For

When you hear the call of
a Red-shouldered Hawk,
American Crow or even
a neighborhood cat, make
sure it is not really a Blue
Jay imitating their calls.

American Crow
Corvus brachyrhynchos

The noise that most often emanates from this treetop squawker seems unrepresentative of its intelligence. However, this wary, clever bird is also an impressive mimic, able to whine like a dog and laugh or cry like a human. • American Crows have flourished in spite of considerable efforts over many generations to reduce their numbers. One of the reasons for this species' staying power is that it is a generalist, which allows it to adapt to a variety of habitats, food types and changing environmental conditions.

Other ID: glossy, purple-black plumage; black bill and legs.
Size: *L* 17–21 in; *W* 3 ft.
Voice: distinctive, far-carrying, repetitive *caw-caw-caw*.
Status: abundant permanent resident statewide.
Habitat: urban areas, agricultural fields and other open areas with scattered woodlands.

Similar Birds

Fish Crow

Common Grackle

Common Raven

slim, sleek head
and throat

square-shaped tail

Nesting: in a tree or on a utility pole; large
stick-and-branch nest is lined with fur and soft
plant materials; darkly blotched, gray-green to
blue-green eggs are 1⅝ x 1⅛ in; female incubates
4–6 eggs for about 18 days.

Did You Know?

Crows are family oriented,
and the young from the
previous year may help
their parents to raise the
nestlings.

Look For

Crows often drop walnuts
and clams from a great height
onto a hard surface to crack
the shells, one of the few
examples of birds using
objects to manipulate food.

Purple Martin
Progne subis

In return for you setting up luxurious "condo complexes" for these large swallows, they will entertain you throughout spring and summer. Martin adults spiral around their accommodations in pursuit of flying insects, while their young perch clumsily at the cavity openings. Purple Martins once nested in natural tree hollows and in cliff crevices, but now have virtually abandoned these in favor of human-made housing. • To avoid the invasion of aggressive House Sparrows or European Starlings, it is essential for martin condos to be cleaned out and closed up after each nesting season.

Other ID: pointed wings; small bill.
Size: *L* 7–8 in; *W* 18 in.
Voice: rich, fluty, robinlike *pew-pew,* often heard in flight.
Status: common summer resident statewide; less common in mountains.
Habitat: semi-open areas, often near water.

Similar Birds

European Starling
(p. 146)

Barn Swallow
(p. 126)

Tree Swallow
(p. 124)

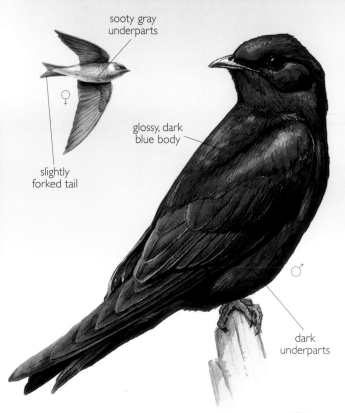

sooty gray
underparts

♀

glossy, dark
blue body

slightly
forked tail

♂

dark
underparts

Nesting: communal; in a human-made birdhouse
or hollowed-out gourd; nest is made of feathers,
grass and mud; white eggs are 1 x ⅝ in; female
incubates 4–5 eggs for 15–18 days.

Did You Know?

The Purple Martin is
North America's largest
swallow.

Look For

Purple Martins can be seen at
martin condo complexes that
are erected in open areas,
high on a pole and near a
body of water.

Tree Swallow
Tachycineta bicolor

Tree Swallows are expanding their range into Virginia and are usually seen perched beside fence-post nest boxes erected for bluebirds. When conditions are favorable, these busy birds are known to return to their young 10 to 20 times per hour—about 140 to 300 times a day! This nearly ceaseless activity provides observers with plenty of opportunities to watch and photograph these birds in action. • In the evening and during light rains, small groups of foraging Tree Swallows sail gracefully above rivers and wetlands, catching stoneflies, mayflies and caddisflies.

Other ID: no white on "cheek." *Female:* slightly duller. *In flight:* long, pointed wings.
Size: *L* 5½ in; *W* 14½ in.
Voice: alarm call is a metallic, buzzy *klweet*. *Male:* song is a liquid, chattering twitter.
Status: locally common summer resident statewide; common migrant; uncommon winter resident at coastal sites.
Habitat: open areas; fencelines with blue-bird nest boxes and fringes of open woodlands, especially near water.

Similar Birds

Purple Martin
(p. 122)

Eastern Kingbird
(p. 112)

Barn Swallow
(p. 126)

small bill

iridescent, dark
blue or green head
and upperparts

white
underparts

shallowly
forked tail

Nesting: in a tree cavity or nest box lined with
weeds, grass and feathers; white eggs are ¾ x ½ in;
female incubates 4–6 eggs for up to 19 days.

Did You Know?

When Tree Swallows leave
the nest to forage, they
frequently cover their eggs
with feathers from the
nest lining.

Look For

In the bright sunshine, the
Tree Swallow's back appears
blue; prior to fall migration,
the back appears green.

Barn Swallow
Hirundo rustica

When you encounter this bird, you might first notice its distinctive, deeply forked tail—or you might just find yourself repeatedly ducking to avoid the dives of a protective parent. Barn Swallows once nested on cliffs, but they are now found more frequently nesting on barns, boathouses and areas under bridges and house eaves. Unfortunately, the messy young and aggressive parents often motivate people to remove nests just as nesting season is beginning, but this bird's close association with humans allows us to observe the normally secretive reproductive cycle of birds.

Other ID: blue-black upperparts; long, pointed wings.
Size: L 7 in; W 15 in.
Voice: continuous, twittering chatter: *zip-zip-zip* or *kvick-kvick*.
Status: common summer resident and migrant statewide.
Habitat: open rural and urban areas where bridges, culverts and buildings are found near water.

Similar Birds

Cliff Swallow

Purple Martin
(p. 122)

Tree Swallow
(p. 124)

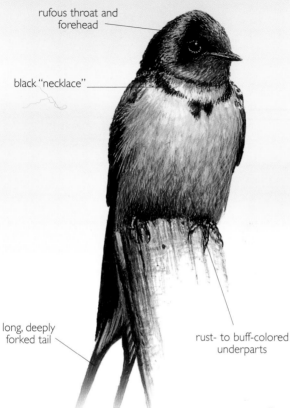

rufous throat and forehead

black "necklace"

long, deeply forked tail

rust- to buff-colored underparts

Nesting: singly or in small, loose colonies; on a human-made structure under an overhang; half or full cup nest is made of mud, grass and straw; brown-spotted, white eggs are ¾ x ½ in; pair incubates 4–7 eggs for 13–17 days.

Did You Know?

The Barn Swallow is a natural pest controller, feeding on insects that are often harmful to crops and livestock.

Look For

Barn Swallows roll mud into small balls and build their nests one mouthful of mud at a time.

Carolina Chickadee
Poecile carolinensis

Fidgety, friendly Carolina Chickadees are familiar to anyone with a backyard feeder well stocked with sunflower seeds and peanut butter. These agile birds even hang upside down to pluck up insects and berries. Like some woodpeckers and nuthatches, the Carolina Chickadee will hoard food for later in the season when food may become scarce. • Come breeding season, this energetic little bird can be found hammering out a nesting cavity in a rotting tree. Occasionally, a chickadee will nest in an abandoned woodpecker hole or birdhouse. • Where the ranges of the Carolina Chickadee and the Black-capped Chickadee *(P. atricapillus)* overlap in the Appalachians, the Carolina Chickadee tends to stick to lower elevations.

Other ID: white cheeks; buffy flanks.
Size: L 4¾ in; W 7½ in.
Voice: whistling song has 4 clear notes: *fee-bee fee-bay.*
Status: common permanent resident statewide, except less common in plateau region of mountains.
Habitat: deciduous and mixed woods, riparian woodlands, groves and isolated shade trees; frequents urban areas.

Similar Birds

Black-capped
Chickadee

White-breasted
Nuthatch (p. 130)

Blackpoll Warbler

black cap and "bib"

grayish nape

gray upperparts
and secondaries

white
underparts

Nesting: excavates or enlarges a tree cavity; may also use nest box; cavity is lined with soft material; white eggs, marked with reddish brown, are 9/16 x 7/16 in; female incubates 5–8 eggs for 11–14 days.

Did You Know?

Each fall, adult Carolina Chickadees tour the neighborhood, introducing their offspring to the best feeding spots.

Look For

Alert Carolina Chickadees are often the first to issue alarm calls, warning other birds that danger is near.

White-breasted Nuthatch
Sitta carolinensis

Its upside-down antics and noisy, nasal call make the White-breasted Nuthatch a favorite among novice birders. Whether you spot this black-capped bullet spiraling headfirst down a tree or clinging to the underside of a branch in search of invertebrates, the nuthatch's odd behavior deserves a second glance. • Comparing the White-breasted Nuthatch to the Carolina Chickadee, both regular visitors to backyard feeders, is a perfect starting point for introductory birding. Both species have dark crowns and gray backs, but the nuthatch's foraging behaviors and undulating flight pattern are distinctive.

Other ID: white underparts; straight bill; short legs.
Size: *L* 5½–6 in; *W* 11 in.
Voice: song is a fast, nasal *yank-hank yank-hank*, lower than the Red-breasted Nuthatch; calls include *ha-ha-ha ha-ha-ha, ank ank* and *ip*.
Status: common permanent resident statewide; less common in the lower Coastal Plain.
Habitat: mixedwood forests, woodlots and backyards.

Similar Birds

Red-breasted Nuthatch

Carolina Chickadee
(p. 128)

Brown Creeper

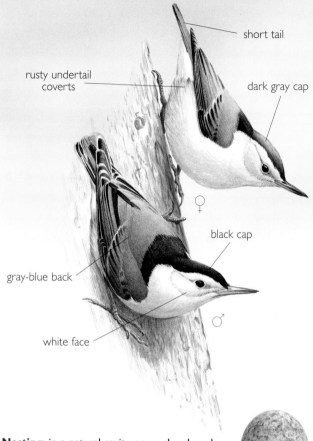

short tail

rusty undertail coverts

dark gray cap

♀

black cap

gray-blue back

♂

white face

Nesting: in a natural cavity or an abandoned woodpecker nest; female lines the cavity with soft material; brown-speckled, white eggs are ¾ x ⁹⁄₁₆ in; female incubates 5–8 eggs for 12–14 days.

Did You Know?

Nuthatches are presumably named for their habit of wedging seeds and nuts into crevices and hacking them open with their bills.

Look For

Woodpeckers use their tails to brace themselves against tree trunks, but nuthatches grasp the tree through foot power alone.

Carolina Wren
Thryothorus ludovicianus

The energetic, cheerful Carolina Wren can be
shy and retiring, often hiding deep inside dense
shrubbery. The best opportunity for viewing this
large wren is when it sits on a conspicuous perch
unleashing its impressive song. Pairs perform lively
"duets" at any time of day and in any season. The
duet often begins with introductory chatter by the
female, followed by innumerable ringing variations
of *tea-kettle tea-kettle tea-kettle tea* from her mate.
• Carolina Wrens readily nest in the brushy thickets
of an overgrown backyard or in an obscure nook
or crevice in a house or barn. If conditions are
favorable, a female may raise two broods in a
single season.

Other ID: white throat; slightly downcurved bill.
Size: L 5½ in; W 7½ in.
Voice: loud, repetitious *tea-kettle tea-kettle tea-kettle
tea* may be heard at any time of day or year; female
often chatters while male sings.
Status: common permanent resident statewide.
Habitat: dense forest undergrowth,
especially shrubby tangles and thickets.

Similar Birds

House Wren

Winter Wren

Marsh Wren

long, prominent,
white "eyebrow"

rusty brown
upperparts

rich buff-colored
underparts

Nesting: in a nest box or natural or artificial cavity; nest is lined with soft materials and may include a snakeskin; brown-blotched, white eggs are ¾ x ⁹/₁₆ in; female incubates 4–5 eggs for 12–16 days.

Did You Know?

In mild winters, Carolina Wren populations remain stable, but frigid temperatures can temporarily decimate an otherwise healthy population.

Look For

In winter, Carolina Wrens will roost near houses in hanging baskets of ferns or other plants or even in Christmas wreaths.

Eastern Bluebird
Sialia sialis

The Eastern Bluebird's enticing colors are like those of a warm setting sun against a deep blue sky. This cavity nester's survival has been put to the test—populations have declined in the presence of the competitive, introduced House Sparrow and European Starling. The removal of standing dead trees has also diminished nest site availability. Thankfully, bluebird enthusiasts and organizations have developed "bluebird trails"—mounted nest boxes on fence posts along highways and rural roads—that have allowed Eastern Bluebird numbers to gradually recover.

Other ID: dark bill and legs. *Female:* thin, white eye ring; gray-brown head and back tinged with blue; blue wings and tail; paler chestnut underparts.
Size: *L* 7 in; *W* 13 in.
Voice: song is a rich, warbling *turr, turr-lee, turr-lee;* call is a chittering *pew.*
Status: locally common permanent resident statewide.
Habitat: cropland fencelines, meadows, fallow and abandoned fields, pastures, forest clearings and edges, golf courses, large lawns and cemeteries.

Similar Birds

Indigo Bunting
(p. 170)

Blue Grosbeak
(p. 168)

deep blue
upperparts

chestnut red
"chin," throat
and sides

white belly and
undertail coverts

♂

Nesting: in a natural cavity or nest box; female
builds a cup nest of grass, weed stems and small
twigs; pale blue eggs are ⅞ x ⅝ in; female incubates 4–5 eggs for 13–16 days.

Did You Know?

A cold spell in spring can
kill the Eastern Bluebird,
freezing the eggs and the
adult while it sits on
the nest.

Look For

The Eastern Bluebird uses an
elevated perch as a base from
which to hunt insects.

Wood Thrush
Hylocichla mustelina

The loud, warbled notes of the Wood Thrush once resounded through our woodlands, but forest fragmentation and urban sprawl have eliminated much of this bird's nesting habitat. Broken forests and diminutive woodlots have also allowed for the invasion of common, open-area predators and parasites, such as raccoons, skunks, crows, jays and cowbirds. Traditionally these predators had little access to nests that were hidden deep within vast hardwood forests.

Other ID: plump body; streaked "cheeks"; brown wings, rump and tail.
Size: *L* 8 in; *W* 13 in.
Voice: *Male:* bell-like phrases of 3–5 notes, with each note at a different pitch and followed by a trill: *Will you live with me? Way up high in a tree, I'll come right down and…seeee!;* calls include a *pit pit* and *bweebeebeep.*
Status: common summer resident statewide.
Habitat: moist, mature, preferably undisturbed deciduous woodlands and mixed forests.

Similar Birds

American Robin
(p. 138)

Swainson's Thrush

Veery

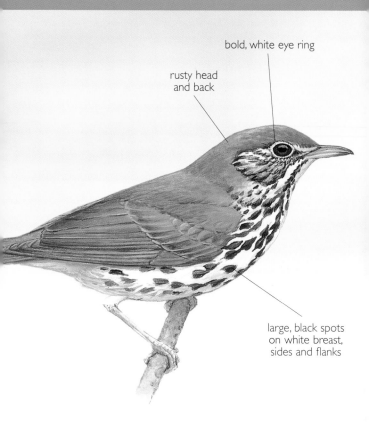

rusty head
and back

bold, white eye ring

large, black spots
on white breast,
sides and flanks

Nesting: low in a fork of a deciduous tree; female builds a bulky cup nest of vegetation, held together with mud and lined with softer materials; pale, greenish blue eggs are 1 x ¾ in; female incubates 3–4 eggs for 13–14 days.

Did You Know?

Henry David Thoreau considered the Wood Thrush's song to be the most beautiful of avian sounds. The male can even sing two notes at once!

Look For

Wood Thrushes forage on the ground or glean vegetation for insects and other invertebrates.

American Robin
Turdus migratorius

Come March, the familiar song of the American Robin may wake you early if you are a light sleeper. This abundant bird adapts easily to urban areas and often works from dawn until after dusk when there is a nest to be built or hungry, young mouths to feed. • The robin's bright red belly contrasts with its dark head and wings, making this bird easy to identify. • In winter, fruit trees may attract flocks of robins, which gather to drink the fermenting fruit's intoxicating juices.

Other ID: incomplete, white eye ring; gray-brown back; white undertail coverts.
Size: L 10 in; W 17 in.
Voice: song is an evenly spaced warble: *cheerily cheer-up cheerio;* call is a rapid *tut-tut-tut.*
Status: common permanent resident statewide; uncommon in the mountains and upper Piedmont in winter.
Habitat: *Breeding:* residential lawns and gardens, pastures, urban parks, broken forests, bogs and river shorelines. *Winter:* near fruit-bearing trees and springs.

Similar Birds

Orchard Oriole

Veery

black head

dark gray head

white throat
is streaked
with black

black-tipped,
yellow bill

♂   ♀

brick red breast is
darker on male

Nesting: in a tree or shrub; cup nest is built of grass, moss, bark and mud; light blue eggs are 1⅛ x ¾ in; female incubates 4 eggs for 11–16 days; raises up to 3 broods per year.

Did You Know?

Robins usually raise two broods per year, and the male cares for the fledglings from the first brood while the female incubates the second clutch of eggs.

Look For

A hunting robin with its head tilted to the side isn't listening for prey—it is actually looking for movements in the soil.

Gray Catbird

Dumetella carolinensis

This accomplished mimic may fool you if you hear it shuffling through underbrush and dense riparian shrubs, calling its catlike *meow*. Its mimicking talents are further enhanced by its ability to sing two notes at once, using each side of its syrinx individually. • In a competitive nesting habitat of sparrows, robins and cowbirds, the Gray Catbird will vigilantly defend its territory. It will destroy the eggs and nestlings of other songbirds and takes on an intense defensive posture if approached, screaming and even attempting to hit an intruder.

Other ID: dark gray overall; black eyes, bill and legs.
Size: *L* 8½–9 in; *W* 11 in.
Voice: calls include a catlike *meow* and a harsh *check-check*; song is a variety of warbles, squeaks and mimicked phrases interspersed with a *mew* call.
Status: common permanent resident at the coast; common breeder and migrant in the mountains and Piedmont.
Habitat: dense thickets, brambles, shrubby or brushy areas and hedgerows, often near water.

Similar Birds

Northern Mockingbird
(p. 142)

Look For

If you catch a glimpse of this bird during breeding season, watch the male raise his long slender tail into the air to show off his rust-colored undertail coverts.

black cap

long tail is dark
gray to black

rust-colored
undertail coverts

Nesting: in a dense shrub or thicket; bulky cup nest is made of twigs, leaves and grass; greenish blue eggs are $7/8$ x $5/8$ in; female incubates 4 eggs for 12–15 days.

Did You Know?

The watchful female Gray Catbird can recognize a Brown-headed Cowbird egg and will remove it from her nest. The ability to recognize the foreign eggs is learned, and only about a dozen species are able to do so.

Northern Mockingbird

Mimus polyglottos

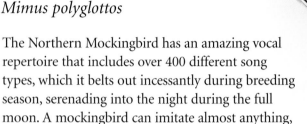

The Northern Mockingbird has an amazing vocal repertoire that includes over 400 different song types, which it belts out incessantly during breeding season, serenading into the night during the full moon. A mockingbird can imitate almost anything, from the vocalizations of other birds and animals to musical instruments. In fact, this bird can replicate sounds so accurately that even computerized auditory analysis is unable to detect the difference between the source and the mockingbird's imitation.

Other ID: gray upperparts; light gray underparts.
In flight: large, white patch at base of black primaries.
Size: L 10 in; W 14 in.
Voice: song is a medley of mimicked phrases, with phrases often repeated 3 times or more; calls include a harsh *chair* and *chewk*.
Status: common permanent resident statewide; less frequent in the mountains.
Habitat: hedges, suburban gardens and orchard margins with an abundance of available fruit; hedgerows of roses are especially important in winter.

Similar Birds

Loggerhead Shrike
(p. 114)

Gray Catbird
(p. 140)

long, dark tail with white outer tail feathers

thin, dark eye line

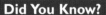

dark wings with 2 thin, white wing bars

Nesting: in a small shrub or small tree; cup nest is built with twigs and plant material; brown-blotched, bluish gray to greenish eggs are 1 x ⅝ in; female incubates 3–4 eggs for 12–13 days.

Did You Know?

The scientific name *polyglottos* is Greek for "many tongues" and refers to this bird's ability to mimic a wide variety of sounds.

Look For

The Northern Mockingbird's energetic territorial dance is delightful to watch as males square off in what appears to be a swordless fencing duel.

Brown Thrasher
Toxostoma rufum

The Brown Thrasher has the streaked breast of a
thrush and the long tail of a catbird, but a temper
all its own. Because it nests close to the ground, the
Brown Thrasher defends its nest with a vengeance,
attacking snakes and other nest robbers, sometimes
to the point of drawing
blood. • Biologists have estimated that the male Brown
Thrasher is capable of producing up to
3000 distinctive song phrases—the most extensive
vocal repertoire of any North American bird.

Other ID: reddish brown upperparts; long, rufous tail;
yellow-orange eyes.
Size: *L* 11½ in; *W* 13 in.
Voice: sings a large variety of phrases, with each phrase
usually repeated twice: *dig-it dig-it, hoe-it hoe-it, pull-it-up
pull-it-up;* calls include a loud crackling note, a harsh
shuck, a soft *churr* or a whistled, 3-note *pit-cher-ee.*
Status: common breeder statewide; uncommon in the
mountains in winter.
Habitat: dense shrubs and thickets, overgrown
pastures, woodland edges and brushy
areas; rarely close to urban areas.

Similar Birds

Hermit Thrush

Wood Thrush
(p. 136)

long, downcurved bill

gray "cheek"

2 white wing bars

pale underparts with heavy, brown streaking

Nesting: usually in a low shrub; often on the ground; cup nest of grass, twigs and leaves is lined with vegetation; pale blue eggs, speckled with reddish brown, are 1 x ¾ in; pair incubates 4 eggs for 11–14 days.

Did You Know?

Shrubby, wooded areas bordering wetlands and streams can be fenced to prevent cattle from devastating thrasher nesting habitat.

Look For

The Brown Thrasher can be hard to find in its shrubby understory habitat. You might catch only a flash of rufous as it flies from one thicket to another.

European Starling

Sturnus vulgaris

The European Starling did not hesitate to make itself known across North America after being released in New York's Central Park in 1890 and 1891. This highly adaptable bird not only took over the nest sites of native cavity nesters, such as Tree Swallows and Red-headed Woodpeckers, but it also learned to mimic the sounds of Killdeers, Red-tailed Hawks, Soras and meadowlarks. • Look for European Starlings in massive evening roosts under bridges or on buildings in winter.

Other ID: dark eyes; short, squared tail.
Nonbreeding: feather tips are heavily spotted with white and buff.
Size: *L* 8½ in; W 16 in.
Voice: variety of whistles, squeaks and gurgles; imitates other birds.
Status: common permanent resident statewide.
Habitat: cities, towns, residential areas, farmyards, woodland fringes and clearings.

Similar Birds

Rusty Blackbird

Brewer's Blackbird

Brown-headed
Cowbird (p. 176)

iridescent, purple-black
head, neck and breast

yellow bill

glossy, green back
with buffy spots

greenish black
underparts

breeding

Nesting: in an abandoned woodpecker hole, natural cavity or nest box; nest is made of grass, twigs and straw; bluish to greenish white eggs are 1⅛ x ⅞ in; female incubates 4–6 eggs for 12–14 days.

Did You Know?

This bird was brought to New York as part of the local Shakespeare society's plan to introduce all the birds mentioned in their favorite author's writings.

Look For

Sometimes confused with a blackbird, the European Starling has a shorter tail and a bright yellow bill.

Cedar Waxwing
Bombycilla cedrorum

With its black "mask" and slick hairdo, the Cedar Waxwing has a heroic look. This bird's splendid personality is reflected in its amusing antics after it gorges on fermented berries and in its gentle courtship dance. To court a mate, the gentlemanly male hops toward a female and offers her a berry. The female accepts the berry and hops away, then stops and hops back toward the male to offer him the berry in return. • If a bird's crop is full and it is unable to eat any more, it will continue to pluck fruit and pass it down the line like a bucket brigade, until the fruit is gulped down by a still-hungry bird.

Other ID: brown upperparts; yellow wash on belly; gray rump.
Size: *L* 7 in; *W* 12 in.
Voice: faint, high-pitched, trilled whistle: *tseee-tseee-tseee.*
Status: widespread but locally common to rare statewide, especially in winter months.
Habitat: wooded residential parks and gardens, overgrown fields, forest edges, second-growth, riparian and open woodlands; often near fruit trees and water.

Similar Birds

Bohemian Waxwing

Look For

The Cedar Waxwing has white undertail coverts, while those of the Bohemian Waxwing are brown.

cinnamon crest

black "mask"

small red "drops" on wings

white undertail coverts

yellow terminal tail band

Nesting: in a tree or shrub; cup nest is made of twigs, moss and lichen; darkly spotted, bluish to gray eggs are ⅞ x ⅝ in; female incubates 3–5 eggs for 12–16 days.

Did You Know?

The yellow tail band and "waxy" red wing tips of the Cedar Waxwing get their color from pigments in the berries that these birds eat.

Common Yellowthroat

Geothlypis trichas

The bumblebee colors of the male Common
Yellowthroat's black "mask" and yellow throat
identify this skulking wetland resident. The cattail
outposts from which he perches to sing his
witchety song are strategically chosen, and he visits
them in rotation, fiercely guarding his territory
against the intrusion of other males. • The
Common Yellowthroat is different from most
wood-warblers, preferring marshlands and wet,
overgrown meadows to forests. The female has no
"mask" and remains mostly hidden from view in
thick vegetation when she tends to the nest.

Other ID: black bill; orangy legs.
Size: L 5 in; W 7 in.
Voice: song is a clear, oscillating *witchety witchety
witchety-witch;* call is a sharp *tcheck* or *tchet.*
Status: common breeder and migrant statewide;
winter resident in the Coastal Plain.
Habitat: coastal areas; wetlands, riparian
areas and wet, overgrown meadows;
sometimes dry fields.

Similar Birds

Wilson's Warbler

Nashville Warbler

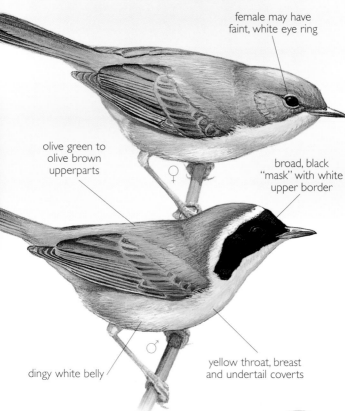

female may have faint, white eye ring

olive green to olive brown upperparts

♀

broad, black "mask" with white upper border

♂

dingy white belly

yellow throat, breast and undertail coverts

Nesting: on or near the ground or in a small shrub or emergent vegetation; female builds an open cup nest of weeds, grass, bark strips and moss; brown-blotched, white eggs are ⅝ x ½ in; female incubates 3–5 eggs for 12 days.

Did You Know?

Famous Swedish biologist Carl Linnaeus named the Common Yellowthroat in 1766, making it one of the first North American birds to be described.

Look For

Common Yellowthroats immerse themselves or roll in water, then shake off the excess water by flicking or flapping their wings.

Pine Warbler
Dendroica pinus

This unassuming bird is perfectly named because it is bound to Virginia's majestic, sheltering pines. Pine Warblers are often difficult to find because they typically forage near the top of very tall, mature pine trees. They are particularly attracted to white and red pines and avoid those with shorter needles. • The Pine Warbler's modest appearance is very similar to a number of immature and fall-plumaged vireos and warblers, forcing birders to obtain a good, long look before making a positive identification. This warbler is most often confused with the Yellow-throated Vireo *(Vireo flavifrons)* or the Bay-breasted Warbler *(D. castanea)* in drab fall plumage.

ID: olive green head and back; dark grayish wings and tail; whitish to dusky wing bars; yellow throat and breast; female duller.
Size: L 5–5 ½ in; W 8 ½ in.
Voice: song is a short, musical trill; call note is a sweet *chip*.
Status: common permanent resident statewide; becoming less common in winter.
Habitat: *Breeding:* open, mature pine woodlands and mature pine plantations. *In migration:* mixed and deciduous woodlands.

Similar Birds

Prairie Warbler

Yellow-throated Vireo

Bay-breasted Warbler

faint, dark line through eye

faint broken yellow eye ring

♀

white undertail coverts and belly

♂

breeding

faded dark streaking or dusky wash on sides of breast

Nesting: near the end of a pine limb; deep, open cup nest of plant material and spider webs is lined with feathers; brown-marked, whitish eggs are 1¾ x 1⅜ in; pair incubates 3–5 eggs for 12–13 days.

Did You Know?

In winter, Pine Warblers will visit bird feeders that offer peanut butter, nuts or cracked corn.

Look For

Occasionally, foraging Pine Warblers can be seen smeared with patches of sticky pine resin.

Yellow-breasted Chat

Icteria virens

At a length of nearly 8 inches, the Yellow-breasted Chat is quite literally a "warbler and a half." Its bright yellow coloration and intense curiosity are all typical warbler traits, but the chat's large size, curious vocalizations and noisy thrashing behavior suggest a closer relationship to the mimic thrushes.
• When much of eastern North America was logged in the early 1900s, the Yellow-breasted Chat became one of our most common breeding birds. Populations have since declined as woodlands mature and shrubby riparian habitat has been lost to development.

Other ID: white jaw line; heavy, black bill; gray-black legs. *Female:* gray lores.
Size: L 7½ in; W 9¾ in.
Voice: single notes or phrases of slurred, piping whistles, *kuks*, harsh rattles and "laughs"; persistent night singing in spring.
Status: common summer resident statewide; less common in southeastern Virginia in Tidewater.
Habitat: dense riparian thickets bordering streams, small ponds and swampy ground; may breed in extensive hillside bramble patches.

Look For

During courtship, a male chat advertises for a mate by launching off his perch, hovering with his head held high and his legs dangling and chirping incessantly.

white "spectacles"

black lores

olive green upperparts

yellow breast

♂

white undertail coverts

Nesting: low in a shrub or a small tree; well-concealed, bulky nest is made of leaves, straw and weeds, with a tight inner cup woven from bark and plant fibers; darkly spotted, creamy white eggs are ⅞ x ⅝ in; female incubates 3–4 eggs for about 11 days.

Did You Know?

Often heard but difficult to see, this elusive bird avoids detection by skulking through brushy riparian thickets and tangled fencerows. On average, a male chat sings 60 different songs and is most vocal early in the breeding season.

Scarlet Tanager
Piranga olivacea

The vibrant red of a breeding male Scarlet Tanager may catch your eye in Virginia's wooded ravines and migrant stopover sites. Because this tanager is more likely to reside in forest canopies, birders tend to hear the Scarlet Tanager before they see it. Its song, a sort of slurred version of the American Robin's, is a much-anticipated sound that announces the arrival of this colorful long-distance migrant. The Scarlet Tanager has the northernmost breeding grounds and longest migration route of all tanager species.

Other ID: *Female:* yellow underparts; grayish brown wings; yellow eye ring.
Size: *L* 7 in; *W* 11½ in.
Voice: song is a series of 4–5 sweet, clear, whistled phrases; call is *chip-burrr* or *chip-churrr*.
Status: common summer resident and migrant statewide.
Habitat: fairly mature, upland deciduous and mixed forests; also coastal shrubbery in migration.

Similar Birds

Summer Tanager

Northern Cardinal
(p. 166)

uniformly olive
upperparts

pale bill

♀

♂

pure black
wings and tail

bright red body

breeding

Nesting: high in a deciduous tree; female builds a flimsy, shallow cup nest of grass, weeds and twigs; brown-spotted, pale blue-green eggs are ⅞ x ⅝ in; female incubates 2–5 eggs for 12–14 days.

Did You Know?

In Central and South America, there are over 200 tanager species in every color imaginable.

Look For

Scarlet Tanagers forage in the forest understory in cold, rainy weather, making them easier to observe.

Eastern Towhee
Pipilo erythrophthalmus

Eastern Towhees are large, colorful members of the sparrow family. These noisy birds are often heard before they are seen as they rustle about in dense undergrowth, craftily scraping back layers of dry leaves to expose the seeds, berries or insects hidden beneath. They employ an unusual two-footed technique to uncover food items—a strategy that is especially important in winter when virtually all of their food is taken from the ground. • The Eastern Towhee and its similar western relative, the Spotted Towhee *(P. maculatus)*, were once grouped together as a single species called the "Rufous-sided Towhee."

Other ID: buff undertail coverts; eyes commonly red, but in southeastern U.S. may be white or orange.
Size: L 7–8½ in; W 10½ in.
Voice: song is 2 high, whistled notes followed by a trill: *drink your teeeee;* call is a scratchy, slurred *cheweee!* or *chewink!*
Status: common permanent resident statewide, but less common in winter.
Habitat: along woodland edges; shrubby, abandoned fields and residential areas.

Similar Birds

Dark-eyed Junco
(p. 164)

Look For

Showy towhees are easily attracted to feeders, where they scratch on the ground for millet, oats or sunflower seeds.

black back, "hood" and bill

brown "hood" and upperparts

small, white wing patch

♂

white outer tail corners

rufous sides and flanks

♀

white lower breast and belly

Nesting: on the ground or low in a dense shrub; female builds a cup nest of twigs, bark strips, grass and animal hair; brown-speckled, creamy white to grayish eggs are $7/8$ x $5/8$ in; mainly the female incubates 3–4 eggs for 12–13 days.

Did You Know?

The scientific name *erythrophthalmus* means "red eye" in Greek, though towhees in the southeastern states may have white or orange irises.

Song Sparrow

Melospiza melodia

Although its plumage is unremarkable, the well-named Song Sparrow is among the great singers of the bird world. When a young male Song Sparrow is only a few months old, he has already created a courtship tune of his own, having learned the basics of melody and rhythm from his father and rival males. • In winter, adaptable Song Sparrows are common throughout Virginia and inhabit woodland edges, weedy ditches and riparian thickets. They regularly visit backyard feeders, belting out their sweet, three-part song throughout the year.

Other ID: white jaw line with dark "mustache" stripes; mottled brown upperparts; rounded tail tip.
Size: *L* 6–7 in; *W* 8 in.
Voice: song is 1–4 introductory notes, such as *sweet sweet sweet,* followed by buzzy *towee,* then a short, descending trill; call is short *tsip* or *tchep.*
Status: common permanent resident statewide.
Habitat: willow shrub lands, riparian thickets, forest openings and pastures, all often near water.

Similar Birds

Swamp Sparrow

Fox Sparrow

Seaside Sparrow

brown line behind eye

dark crown with pale central stripe

grayish face

heavy brown streaks converge at central breast spot

Nesting: usually on the ground or in a low shrub; female builds an open cup nest of grass, weeds and bark strips; brown-blotched, greenish white eggs are ⅞ x ⅝ in; female incubates 3–5 eggs for 12–14 days.

Did You Know?

Though female songbirds are not usually vocal, the female Song Sparrow will occasionally sing a tune of her own.

Look For

The Song Sparrow pumps its long, rounded tail in flight. It also often issues a high-pitched *seet* flight call.

White-throated Sparrow

Zonotrichia albicollis

The White-throated Sparrow belts out its distinctive melody year-round, and is one of the easiest sparrows to learn and identify. Its bold, white throat and striped crown can only be confused with White-crowned Sparrow *(Z. leucophrys)*, but the two birds favor different habitats. White-throats usually stick to forested woodlands, while White-crowns prefer open, bushy habitats and farmlands. • Two color morphs are common: one has black and white head stripes; the other has brown and tan stripes.

Other ID: gray "cheek"; black eye line; unstreaked, gray underparts; mottled brown upperparts.
Size: L 6½–7½ in; W 9 in.
Voice: variable song is a clear, distinct, whistled: *Old Sam Peabody, Peabody, Peabody;* call is a sharp *chink.*
Status: common winter resident and migrant statewide.
Habitat: woodlots; wooded parks and riparian brush.

Similar Birds

White-crowned
Sparrow

Swamp Sparrow

yellow lores

black and white
(or brown and tan)
head stripes

white throat

grayish bill

white-striped morph

Nesting: does not nest in Virginia; nests in Great Lakes area and Canada; on or near the ground; open cup nest of plant material is lined with fine grass and hair; variably marked, bluish eggs are $7/8$ x $9/16$ in; female incubates 4–5 eggs for 11–14 days.

Did You Know?

Zonotrichia means "hair-like," a reference to the striped heads of birds in this genus.

Look For

During migration, White-throated Sparrows forage mostly on the ground. They kick aside leaf litter and pounce on the insects they find underneath.

Dark-eyed Junco

Junco hyemalis

Dark-eyed Juncos usually congregate in backyards with bird feeders and sheltering conifers—with such amenities at their disposal, more and more juncos are appearing in urban areas. Juncos spend most of their time on the ground, snatching up seeds underneath bird feeders, and they are readily flushed from wooded trails and backyard feeders. Their distinctive, white outer tail feathers flash in alarm as they seek cover in a nearby tree or shrub. • The junco is often called the "Snow Bird," and the species name *hyemalis* means "winter" in Greek.

Other ID: *Female:* gray-brown where male is slate gray.
Size: *L* 6–7 in; *W* 9 in.
Voice: song is a long, dry trill; call is a smacking *chip* note, often given in series.
Status: common breeder in mountains; common migrant and winter resident statewide.
Habitat: shrubby woodland borders, backyard feeders.

Similar Birds

Eastern Towhee
(p. 158)

Look For

When an incubating female is flushed from her nest, she runs along the ground with her wings extended instead of flying away.

pale pink bill

dark slate
gray overall

white outer
tail feathers

♂

white belly and
undertail coverts

"Slate-colored Junco"

Nesting: on the ground or in a shrub or tree, usually concealed; female builds a cup nest of twigs, grass, bark shreds and moss; brown-marked, whitish to bluish eggs are ¾ x ½ in; female incubates 3–5 eggs for 12–13 days.

Did You Know?

There are five closely related Dark-eyed Junco subspecies in North America that share similar habits but differ in coloration and range.

Northern Cardinal
Cardinalis cardinalis

An excited or agitated male Northern Cardinal will display his unforgettable, vibrant red head crest and raise his tail. This colorful year-round resident will vigorously defend his territory, even attacking his own reflection in a window or hubcap! • Cardinals are one of only a few bird species to maintain strong pair bonds. Some couples sing to each other year-round, while others join loose flocks, reestablishing pair bonds in the spring during a "courtship feeding." A male offers a seed to the female, which she then accepts and eats. • The Northern Cardinal is Virginia's official state bird.

Other ID: *Male:* red overall. *Female:* brownish buff overall; fainter "mask"; red crest, wings and tail.
Size: *L* 8–9 in; *W* 12 in.
Voice: call is a metallic *chip;* song is series of clear, bubbly whistled notes: *What cheer! What cheer! birdie-birdie-birdie what cheer!*
Status: common permanent resident statewide.
Habitat: brushy thickets and shrubby tangles along forest and woodland edges; backyards and urban and suburban parks.

Similar Birds

Summer Tanager

Scarlet Tanager
(p. 156)

pointed crest

conical red bill

black "mask" and throat

♀

♂

Nesting: in a dense shrub or vine tangle, or low in a coniferous tree; female builds an open cup nest of twigs, grass and bark shreds; brown-blotched, white to greenish white eggs are 1 x ¾ in; female incubates 3–4 eggs for 12–13 days.

Did You Know?

This bird owes its name to the vivid red plumage of the male, which resembles the robes of Roman Catholic cardinals.

Look For

Northern Cardinals fly with jerky movements and short glides and have a preference for sunflower seeds.

Blue Grosbeak
Passerina caerulea

Male Blue Grosbeaks owe their spectacular spring plumage not to a fresh molt but, oddly enough, to feather wear. While Blue Grosbeaks are wintering in Mexico or Central America, their brown feather tips slowly wear away, leaving the crystal blue plumage that is seen as they arrive on their breeding grounds. The lovely blue color is produced by tiny particles in the feathers that reflect only short wavelengths in the light spectrum. • Blue Grosbeaks are very expressive during courtship. In spring, watch for the tail-spreading, tail-flicking and crown-raising behaviors that suggest the birds might be breeding.

Other ID: *Male:* black around base of bill. *Female:* whitish throat; rump and shoulders faintly washed with blue.
Size: L 6–7½ in; W 11 in.
Voice: sweet, melodious, warbling song with phrases that rise and fall; call is a loud *chink*
Status: common summer resident and migrant in the Piedmont, Coastal Plain and valleys; less common to absent from the mountains.
Habitat: thick brush, riparian thickets, shrubby areas and dense weedy fields near water.

Similar Birds

Indigo Bunting
(p. 170)

Look For

A pair of rusty wing bars distinguish the Blue Grosbeak from the similar-looking and much more common Indigo Bunting.

blue overall

2 rusty wing bars

stubby, pale grayish
conical bill

soft brown plumage

♂

♀

long tail

Nesting: in a shrub or low tree; cup nest is
woven with twigs, roots and grass and lined with
finer material, including paper and occasionally
a shed reptile skin; pale blue eggs are ⅞ x ⅝ in;
female incubates 2–5 eggs for 11–12 days.

Did You Know?

Caerulea is from the Latin for "blue," a description that just
doesn't express this bird's true beauty. At a distance, the
male's striking plumage may look blackish.

Indigo Bunting

Passerina cyanea

The vivid electric blue male Indigo Bunting is one of the most spectacular birds in Virginia. These birds arrive in April or May and favor raspberry thickets as nest sites. Dense, thorny stems keep most predators at a distance and the berries are a good food source. • The male is a persistent singer, vocalizing even through the heat of a summer day. A young male doesn't learn his couplet song from his parents, but from neighboring males during his first year on his own. • Planting coneflower, cosmos or foxtail grasses may attract Indigo Buntings to your backyard.

Other ID: beady black eyes; black legs; no wing bars. *Male:* bright blue overall; black lores. *Female:* soft brown overall; whitish throat.
Size: L 5½ in; W 8 in.
Voice: song consists of paired warbled whistles: *fire-fire, where-where, here-here, see-it see-it;* call is a quick *spit.*
Status: common summer resident and migrant statewide.
Habitat: deciduous forest and woodland edges, regenerating forest clearings, orchards and shrubby fields.

Similar Birds

Blue Grosbeak
(p. 168)

Eastern Bluebird
(p. 134)

darker blue head

gray, conical bill

♂

♀

faint brown streaks on breast

wings and tail may show some black

breeding

Nesting: in a small tree, shrub or within a vine tangle; female builds a cup nest of grass, leaves and bark strips; unmarked, white to bluish white eggs are ¾ x ½ in; female incubates 3–4 eggs for 12–13 days.

Did You Know?

Females choose the most melodious males as mates, because these males can usually establish territories with the finest habitat.

Look For

The Indigo Bunting will land midway on a stem of grass or a weed and shuffle slowly toward the seed head, bending down the stem to reach the seeds.

Red-winged Blackbird

Agelaius phoeniceus

The male Red-winged Blackbird wears his bright red shoulders like armor—together with his short, raspy song, they are key in defending his territory from rivals. In field experiments, males whose red shoulders were painted black soon lost their territories. • Nearly every cattail marsh worthy of description in Virginia plays host to Red-winged Blackbirds during at least some of the year. • The female's cryptic coloration allows her to sit inconspicuously on her nest, blending in perfectly with the surroundings.

Other ID: *Male:* black overall. *Female:* mottled brown upperparts; pale "eyebrow."
Size: L 7½–9 in; W 13 in.
Voice: song is a loud, raspy *konk-a-ree* or *ogle-reeeee;* calls include a harsh *check* and high *tseert;* female gives a loud *che-che-che chee chee chee.*
Status: common breeder and migrant statewide; more common at the coast in winter.
Habitat: cattail marshes, wet meadows and ditches, croplands and shoreline shrubs.

Similar Birds

Brewer's Blackbird

Rusty Blackbird

Brown-headed Cowbird (p. 176)

faint, red
shoulder patch

♂

heavily streaked
underparts

♀

red shoulder
patch edged
in yellow

Nesting: colonial; in cattails or shoreline bushes; female builds an open cup nest of dried cattail leaves lined with fine grass; darkly marked, pale bluish green eggs are 1 x ¾ in; female incubates 3–4 eggs for 10–12 days.

Did You Know?

Some scientists believe that the Red-winged Blackbird is the most abundant bird species in North America.

Look For

As he sings his *konk-a-ree* song, the male Red-winged Blackbird spreads his shoulders to display his bright red epaulets to rivals and potential mates.

Eastern Meadowlark
Sturnella magna

The drab dress of most female songbirds lends them and their nestlings protection during the breeding season, but the female Eastern Meadowlark uses a different strategy. Her "V" necklace and bright yellow throat and belly create a colorful distraction as she leads predators away from the nest. A female flushed from the nest while incubating her eggs will often abandon the nest, and though she will never abandon her chicks, her extra vigilance following a threat usually results in less frequent feeding of nestlings.

Other ID: yellow underparts; mottled brown upperparts; long, sharp bill; pale "eyebrow" and median crown stripe; blackish crown stripes and eye line; long, pinkish legs.
Size: *L* 9–9½ in; *W* 14 in.
Voice: song is a rich series of 2–8 melodic, clear, slurred whistles: *see-you at school-today* or *this is the year;* gives a rattling flight call and a high, buzzy *dzeart.*
Status: locally common permanent resident statewide.
Habitat: grassy meadows and pastures, croplands, grassy roadsides; old orchards; also coastal barrens in migration and winter.

Similar Birds

Dickcissel

Look For

The Eastern Meadowlark often whistles its proud song from fence posts and power lines. Song is the best way to tell it apart from the extremely rare Western Meadowlark.

white jaw line

dark streaking on
white sides and flanks

broad, black
breast band

short, wide tail
with white outer
tail feathers

breeding

Nesting: in a concealed depression on the
ground; female builds a domed grass nest, woven
into surrounding vegetation; darkly marked, white
eggs are 1⅛ x ¾ in; female incubates 3–7 eggs
for 13–15 days.

Did You Know?

Though the name suggests that this bird is a lark, it is actually
a brightly colored member of the blackbird family. Its silhouette reveals its blackbird features.

Brown-headed Cowbird

Molothrus ater

These nomads historically followed bison herds across the Great Plains (they now follow cattle), so they never stayed in one area long enough to build and tend a nest. Instead, cowbirds lay their eggs in other birds' nests, relying on the unsuspecting adoptive parents to incubate the eggs and feed the aggressive young. Orioles, warblers, vireos and tanagers are among the most affected species. Increased livestock farming and fragmentation of forests has encouraged the expansion of the cowbird's range, and it now parasitizes more than 140 bird species.

Other ID: thick, conical bill; short, squared tail.
Size: *L* 6–8 in; *W* 12 in.
Voice: song is a high, liquidy gurgle: *glug-ahl-whee* or *bubbloozeee;* call is a squeaky, high-pitched *seep, psee* or *wee-tse-tse* or fast, chipping *ch-ch-ch-ch-ch-ch.*
Status: common breeder and migrant; locally abundant in winter especially in the Coastal Plain.
Habitat: agricultural and residential areas, fields, woodland edges, roadsides, landfills and areas near cattle.

Similar Birds

Rusty Blackbird

Brewer's Blackbird

Common Grackle

dark eyes

dark brown head

pale throat

light brown underparts with faint streaking

♀

♂

iridescent, green-blue body plumage looks glossy black

Nesting: does not build a nest; female lays up to 40 eggs a year in the nests of other birds, usually 1 egg per nest; brown-speckled, whitish eggs are $7/8$ x $5/8$ in; eggs hatch after 10–13 days.

Did You Know?

When courting a female, the male cowbird points his bill upward to the sky, fans his tail and wings and utters a loud *squeek.*

Look For

When cowbirds feed in flocks, they hold their back ends up high, with their tails sticking straight up in the air.

Baltimore Oriole
Icterus galbula

With a flutelike song and a preference for the canopies of neighborhood trees, the Baltimore Oriole is difficult to spot, and a hanging pouch nest dangling in a bare tree in fall is sometimes the only evidence that the bird was there at all. The nests are deceptively strong and often remain intact through the harshest winters. • The male's plumage mirrors the colors of the coat of arms of Sir George Calvert, Baron Baltimore, who established the first colony in Maryland.

Other ID: *Female:* olive brown upperparts (darkest on head).
Size: *L* 7–8 in; *W* 11½ in.
Voice: song consists of slow, clear whistles: *peter peter peter here peter;* calls include a 2-note *tea-too* and a rapid chatter: *ch-ch-ch-ch-ch.*
Status: common breeder in mountains, valleys and upper Piedmont; less common to absent from the Coastal Plain and southern Piedmont.
Habitat: deciduous and mixed forests, particularly riparian woodlands, shorelines, roadsides, orchards, gardens and parklands.

Similar Birds

Orchard Oriole

Scarlet Tanager
(p. 156)

black "hood," back, wings and central tail feathers

white wing bar

♀

dull yellow-orange underparts and rump

♂

bright orange under- parts, shoulder, rump and outer tail feathers

Nesting: high in a deciduous tree; female builds a hanging pouch nest of grass, bark shreds and grapevines; darkly marked, pale gray to bluish white eggs are 7/8 x 5/8 in; female incubates 4–5 eggs for 12–14 days.

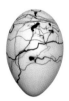

Did You Know?

Orioles spend more than half of each year in the tropics of Central and South America.

Look For

In fall, you can sometimes see a Baltimore Oriole in its Halloween colors at a feeder, especially if orange halves are offered.

American Goldfinch
Carduelis tristis

Like tiny rays of sunshine, American Goldfinches cheerily flutter over weedy fields, gardens and along roadsides. It is hard to miss their jubilant *po-ta-to-chip* call and their distinctive, undulating flight style. • Because these acrobatic birds regularly feed while hanging upside down, finch feeders have been designed with the seed openings below the perches. These feeders discourage the more aggressive House Sparrows, which feed upright, from stealing the seeds. Use niger, millet or black-oil sunflower seeds to attract American Goldfinches to your bird feeder.

Other ID: *Breeding male:* orange bill and legs. *Female:* yellow throat and breast; yellow-green belly. *Nonbreeding male:* olive brown back; yellow-tinged head; gray underparts.
Size: *L* 4½–5 in; *W* 9 in.
Voice: song is a long, varied series of trills, twitters, warbles and hissing notes; calls include *po-ta-to-chip* or *per-chic-or-ee* (often delivered in flight) and a whistled *dear-me, see-me*.
Status: common permanent resident statewide.
Habitat: weedy fields, woodland edges, meadows, riparian areas, parks and gardens.

Similar Birds

Evening Grosbeak

Wilson's Warbler

yellow-green
upperparts

black cap extends
onto forehead

♀

black wings and
tail with white
wing bars

white rump and
undertail coverts

♂

breeding

Nesting: in the fork of a deciduous tree; female builds a compact cup nest of plant fibers, grass and spider silk; unmarked, pale bluish eggs are ⅝ x ½ in; female incubates 4–6 eggs for 12–14 days.

Did You Know?

These birds nest in late summer to ensure that there is a dependable source of seeds from this-tles and dandelions to feed their young.

Look For

American Goldfinches delight in perching on late-summer thistle heads or poking through dandelion patches in search of seeds.

House Sparrow
Passer domesticus

A black "mask" and "bib" adorn the male of this adaptive, aggressive species. The House Sparrow's tendency to usurp territory has led to a decline in native bird populations. This sparrow will even help itself to the convenience of another bird's home, such as a bluebird or Cliff Swallow nest or a Purple Martin house. • This abundant and conspicuous bird was introduced to North America in the 1850s as part of a plan to control the insects that were damaging grain and cereal crops. As it turns out, these birds are largely vegetarian!

Other ID: *Breeding male:* gray crown; black bill; dark, mottled upperparts; gray underparts; white wing bar. *Female:* indistinct facial pattern; plain gray-brown overall; streaked upperparts.
Size: L 5½–6½ in; W 9½ in.
Voice: song is a plain, familiar *cheep-cheep-cheep-cheep;* call is a short *chill-up.*
Status: common permanent resident statewide.
Habitat: townsites, urban and suburban areas, farmyards and agricultural areas, railroad yards and other developed areas.

Similar Birds

Harris's Sparrow

Look For

In spring, House Sparrows feast on the buds of fruit trees. In winter, they flock together in barns in rural areas and at garbage dumps in cities.

buffy "eyebrow"

chestnut nape

light gray "cheek"

♀

black lores and "bib"

breeding

♂

grayish, unstreaked underparts

Nesting: often communal; in a birdhouse, ornamental shrub or natural cavity; pair builds a large dome nest of grass, twigs and plant fibers; gray-speckled, white to greenish eggs are $\frac{7}{8}$ x $\frac{5}{8}$ in; pair incubates 4–6 eggs for 10–13 days.

Did You Know?

The House Sparrow has successfully established itself in North America owing in part to its high reproductive output. A pair may raise up to four clutches per year, with up to six young per clutch.

Glossary

accipiter: a forest hawk (genus *Accipiter*); characterized by a long tail and short, rounded wings; feeds mostly on birds.

brood: *n.* a family of young from one hatching; *v.* to sit on eggs so as to hatch them.

buteo: a high-soaring hawk (genus *Buteo*); characterized by broad wings and short, wide tails; feeds mostly on small mammals and other land animals.

cere: a fleshy area at the base of a bird's bill that contains the nostrils.

clutch: the number of eggs laid by the female at one time.

corvid: a member of the crow family (Corvidae); includes crows, jays, ravens and magpies.

covey: a group of birds, usually grouse or quail.

crop: an enlargement of the esophagus; serves as a storage structure and (in pigeons) has glands that produce secretions.

dabbling: a foraging technique used by ducks, in which the head and neck are submerged but the body and tail remain on the water's surface; dabbling ducks can usually walk easily on land, can take off without running and have brightly colored speculums.

eclipse plumage: a cryptic plumage, similar to that of females, worn by some male ducks in autumn when they molt their flight feathers and consequently are unable to fly.

fledgling: a young bird that has left the nest but is dependent upon its parents.

flushing: a behavior in which frightened birds explode into flight in response to a disturbance.

flycatching: a feeding behavior in which the bird leaves a perch, snatches an insect in midair and returns to the same perch.

hawking: attempting to catch insects through aerial pursuit.

irruptive: when a bird is abundant in some years and almost absent in others.

leading edge: the front edge of the wing as viewed from below.

mantle: feathers of the back and upperside of folded wings.

morph: one of several alternate plumages displayed by members of a species.

niche: an ecological role filled by a species.

nocturnal: active during the night.

pelagic: open ocean habitat very far from land.

polyandry: a mating strategy in which one female breeds with several males.

precocial: a bird that is relatively well developed at hatching; precocial birds usually have open eyes, extensive down and are fairly mobile.

primaries: the outermost flight feathers.

raptor: a carnivorous (meat-eating) bird; includes eagles, hawks, falcons and owls.

riparian: refers to habitat along riverbanks.

rufous: rusty red in color.

sexual dimorphism: a difference in plumage, size, or other characteristics between males and females of the same species.

speculum: a brightly colored patch on the wings of many dabbling ducks.

stoop: a steep dive through the air, usually performed by birds of prey while foraging or during courtship displays.

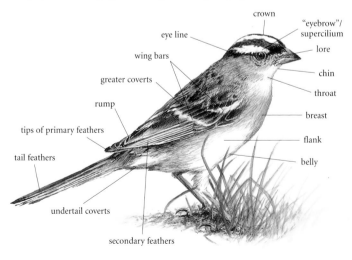

Checklist

The following checklist contains 449 species of birds that have been officially recorded in Virginia. Species are grouped by family and listed in taxonomic order in accordance with the *A.O.U. Check-list of North American Birds* (7th ed.) and its supplements.

We wish to thank the Virginia Avian Records Committee of the Virginia Society of Ornithology for their kind assistance in providing the information for this checklist.

- ❏ Black-bellied Whistling-Duck
- ❏ Fulvous Whistling-Duck
- ❏ Greater White-fronted Goose
- ❏ Snow Goose
- ❏ Ross's Goose
- ❏ Brant
- ❏ Cackling Goose
- ❏ Canada Goose
- ❏ Mute Swan
- ❏ Trumpeter Swan
- ❏ Tundra Swan
- ❏ Wood Duck
- ❏ Gadwall
- ❏ Eurasian Wigeon
- ❏ American Wigeon
- ❏ American Black Duck
- ❏ Mallard
- ❏ Blue-winged Teal
- ❏ Cinnamon Teal
- ❏ Northern Shoveler
- ❏ White-cheeked Pintail
- ❏ Northern Pintail
- ❏ Green-winged Teal
- ❏ Canvasback
- ❏ Redhead
- ❏ Ring-necked Duck
- ❏ Tufted Duck
- ❏ Greater Scaup
- ❏ Lesser Scaup
- ❏ King Eider
- ❏ Common Eider
- ❏ Harlequin Duck
- ❏ Surf Scoter
- ❏ White-winged Scoter
- ❏ Black Scoter
- ❏ Long-tailed Duck
- ❏ Bufflehead
- ❏ Common Goldeneye
- ❏ Barrow's Goldeneye
- ❏ Hooded Merganser
- ❏ Common Merganser
- ❏ Red-breasted Merganser
- ❏ Ruddy Duck
- ❏ Ring-necked Pheasant
- ❏ Ruffed Grouse
- ❏ Wild Turkey
- ❏ Northern Bobwhite
- ❏ Red-throated Loon
- ❏ Pacific Loon
- ❏ Common Loon
- ❏ Pied-billed Grebe
- ❏ Horned Grebe
- ❏ Red-necked Grebe
- ❏ Eared Grebe
- ❏ Western Grebe
- ❏ Clark's Grebe
- ❏ Yellow-nosed Albatross
- ❏ Black-browed Albatross
- ❏ Northern Fulmar
- ❏ Herald Petrel
- ❏ Black-capped Petrel
- ❏ Fea's Petrel
- ❏ Cory's Shearwater
- ❏ Greater Shearwater
- ❏ Sooty Shearwater
- ❏ Short-tailed Shearwater
- ❏ Manx Shearwater
- ❏ Audubon's Shearwater

- ❑ Wilson's Storm-Petrel
- ❑ White-faced Storm-Petrel
- ❑ Leach's Storm-Petrel
- ❑ Band-rumped Storm-Petrel
- ❑ White-tailed Tropicbird
- ❑ Brown Booby
- ❑ Northern Gannet
- ❑ American White Pelican
- ❑ Brown Pelican
- ❑ Double-crested Cormorant
- ❑ Great Cormorant
- ❑ Anhinga
- ❑ Magnificent Frigatebird
- ❑ American Bittern
- ❑ Least Bittern
- ❑ Great Blue Heron
- ❑ Great Egret
- ❑ Little Egret
- ❑ Snowy Egret
- ❑ Little Blue Heron
- ❑ Tricolored Heron
- ❑ Reddish Egret
- ❑ Cattle Egret
- ❑ Green Heron
- ❑ Black-crowned Night-Heron
- ❑ Yellow-crowned Night-Heron
- ❑ White Ibis
- ❑ Glossy Ibis
- ❑ White-faced Ibis
- ❑ Wood Stork
- ❑ Black Vulture
- ❑ Turkey Vulture
- ❑ Greater Flamingo
- ❑ Osprey
- ❑ Swallow-tailed Kite
- ❑ White-tailed Kite
- ❑ Mississippi Kite
- ❑ Bald Eagle
- ❑ Northern Harrier
- ❑ Sharp-shinned Hawk
- ❑ Cooper's Hawk
- ❑ Northern Goshawk
- ❑ Red-shouldered Hawk
- ❑ Broad-winged Hawk
- ❑ Swainson's Hawk
- ❑ Red-tailed Hawk
- ❑ Ferruginous Hawk
- ❑ Rough-legged Hawk
- ❑ Golden Eagle
- ❑ American Kestrel
- ❑ Merlin
- ❑ Gyrfalcon
- ❑ Peregrine Falcon
- ❑ Yellow Rail
- ❑ Black Rail
- ❑ Clapper Rail
- ❑ King Rail
- ❑ Virginia Rail
- ❑ Sora
- ❑ Paint-billed Crake
- ❑ Purple Gallinule
- ❑ Common Moorhen
- ❑ American Coot
- ❑ Limpkin
- ❑ Sandhill Crane
- ❑ Black-bellied Plover
- ❑ American Golden-Plover
- ❑ Snowy Plover
- ❑ Wilson's Plover
- ❑ Semipalmated Plover
- ❑ Piping Plover
- ❑ Killdeer
- ❑ Mountain Plover
- ❑ American Oystercatcher
- ❑ Black-necked Stilt
- ❑ American Avocet
- ❑ Greater Yellowlegs
- ❑ Lesser Yellowlegs
- ❑ Solitary Sandpiper
- ❑ Willet
- ❑ Spotted Sandpiper
- ❑ Upland Sandpiper
- ❑ Whimbrel
- ❑ Long-billed Curlew
- ❑ Hudsonian Godwit
- ❑ Bar-tailed Godwit
- ❑ Marbled Godwit
- ❑ Ruddy Turnstone
- ❑ Red Knot
- ❑ Sanderling
- ❑ Semipalmated Sandpiper
- ❑ Western Sandpiper
- ❑ Red-necked Stint
- ❑ Least Sandpiper
- ❑ White-rumped Sandpiper
- ❑ Baird's Sandpiper

- ❏ Pectoral Sandpiper
- ❏ Sharp-tailed Sandpiper
- ❏ Purple Sandpiper
- ❏ Dunlin
- ❏ Curlew Sandpiper
- ❏ Stilt Sandpiper
- ❏ Buff-breasted Sandpiper
- ❏ Ruff
- ❏ Short-billed Dowitcher
- ❏ Long-billed Dowitcher
- ❏ Wilson's Snipe
- ❏ Eurasian Woodcock
- ❏ American Woodcock
- ❏ Wilson's Phalarope
- ❏ Red-necked Phalarope
- ❏ Red Phalarope
- ❏ Great Skua
- ❏ South Polar Skua
- ❏ Pomarine Jaeger
- ❏ Parasitic Jaeger
- ❏ Long-tailed Jaeger
- ❏ Laughing Gull
- ❏ Franklin's Gull
- ❏ Little Gull
- ❏ Black-headed Gull
- ❏ Bonaparte's Gull
- ❏ Black-tailed Gull
- ❏ Mew Gull
- ❏ Ring-billed Gull
- ❏ California Gull
- ❏ Herring Gull
- ❏ Yellow-legged Gull
- ❏ Thayer's Gull
- ❏ Iceland Gull
- ❏ Lesser Black-backed Gull
- ❏ Glaucous Gull
- ❏ Great Black-backed Gull
- ❏ Sabine's Gull
- ❏ Black-legged Kittiwake
- ❏ Gull-billed Tern
- ❏ Caspian Tern
- ❏ Royal Tern
- ❏ Elegant Tern
- ❏ Sandwich Tern
- ❏ Roseate Tern
- ❏ Common Tern
- ❏ Arctic Tern
- ❏ Forster's Tern
- ❏ Least Tern
- ❏ Bridled Tern
- ❏ Sooty Tern
- ❏ White-winged Tern
- ❏ Black Tern
- ❏ Black Skimmer
- ❏ Dovekie
- ❏ Common Murre
- ❏ Thick-billed Murre
- ❏ Razorbill
- ❏ Black Guillemot
- ❏ Atlantic Puffin
- ❏ Rock Pigeon
- ❏ Eurasian Collared-Dove
- ❏ White-winged Dove
- ❏ Mourning Dove
- ❏ Common Ground-Dove
- ❏ Monk Parakeet
- ❏ Black-billed Cuckoo
- ❏ Yellow-billed Cuckoo
- ❏ Groove-billed Ani
- ❏ Barn Owl
- ❏ Eastern Screech-Owl
- ❏ Great Horned Owl
- ❏ Snowy Owl
- ❏ Burrowing Owl
- ❏ Barred Owl
- ❏ Long-eared Owl
- ❏ Short-eared Owl
- ❏ Northern Saw-whet Owl
- ❏ Common Nighthawk
- ❏ Chuck-will's-widow
- ❏ Whip-poor-will
- ❏ Chimney Swift
- ❏ Magnificent Hummingbird
- ❏ Ruby-throated Hummingbird
- ❏ Black-chinned Hummingbird
- ❏ Anna's Hummingbird
- ❏ Rufous Hummingbird
- ❏ Allen's Hummingbird
- ❏ Belted Kingfisher
- ❏ Lewis's Woodpecker
- ❏ Red-headed Woodpecker
- ❏ Red-bellied Woodpecker
- ❏ Yellow-bellied Sapsucker
- ❏ Downy Woodpecker
- ❏ Hairy Woodpecker
- ❏ Red-cockaded Woodpecker

- ❑ Northern Flicker
- ❑ Pileated Woodpecker
- ❑ Olive-sided Flycatcher
- ❑ Western Wood-Pewee
- ❑ Eastern Wood-Pewee
- ❑ Yellow-bellied Flycatcher
- ❑ Acadian Flycatcher
- ❑ Alder Flycatcher
- ❑ Willow Flycatcher
- ❑ Least Flycatcher
- ❑ Pacific-slope/Cordilleran Flycatcher
- ❑ Eastern Phoebe
- ❑ Say's Phoebe
- ❑ Vermilion Flycatcher
- ❑ Ash-throated Flycatcher
- ❑ Great Crested Flycatcher
- ❑ Western Kingbird
- ❑ Eastern Kingbird
- ❑ Gray Kingbird
- ❑ Scissor-tailed Flycatcher
- ❑ Fork-tailed Flycatcher
- ❑ Loggerhead Shrike
- ❑ Northern Shrike
- ❑ White-eyed Vireo
- ❑ Bell's Vireo
- ❑ Yellow-throated Vireo
- ❑ Blue-headed Vireo
- ❑ Warbling Vireo
- ❑ Philadelphia Vireo
- ❑ Red-eyed Vireo
- ❑ Black-whiskered Vireo
- ❑ Blue Jay
- ❑ Black-billed Magpie
- ❑ American Crow
- ❑ Fish Crow
- ❑ Common Raven
- ❑ Horned Lark
- ❑ Purple Martin
- ❑ Tree Swallow
- ❑ Northern Rough-winged Swallow
- ❑ Bank Swallow
- ❑ Cliff Swallow
- ❑ Cave Swallow
- ❑ Barn Swallow
- ❑ Carolina Chickadee
- ❑ Black-capped Chickadee
- ❑ Boreal Chickadee
- ❑ Tufted Titmouse
- ❑ Red-breasted Nuthatch
- ❑ White-breasted Nuthatch
- ❑ Brown-headed Nuthatch
- ❑ Brown Creeper
- ❑ Rock Wren
- ❑ Carolina Wren
- ❑ Bewick's Wren
- ❑ House Wren
- ❑ Winter Wren
- ❑ Sedge Wren
- ❑ Marsh Wren
- ❑ Golden-crowned Kinglet
- ❑ Ruby-crowned Kinglet
- ❑ Blue-gray Gnatcatcher
- ❑ Northern Wheatear
- ❑ Eastern Bluebird
- ❑ Mountain Bluebird
- ❑ Veery
- ❑ Gray-cheeked Thrush
- ❑ Bicknell's Thrush
- ❑ Swainson's Thrush
- ❑ Hermit Thrush
- ❑ Wood Thrush
- ❑ American Robin
- ❑ Varied Thrush
- ❑ Gray Catbird
- ❑ Northern Mockingbird
- ❑ Sage Thrasher
- ❑ Brown Thrasher
- ❑ European Starling
- ❑ American Pipit
- ❑ Sprague's Pipit
- ❑ Bohemian Waxwing
- ❑ Cedar Waxwing
- ❑ Bachman's Warbler
- ❑ Blue-winged Warbler
- ❑ Golden-winged Warbler
- ❑ Tennessee Warbler
- ❑ Orange-crowned Warbler
- ❑ Nashville Warbler
- ❑ Northern Parula
- ❑ Yellow Warbler
- ❑ Chestnut-sided Warbler
- ❑ Magnolia Warbler
- ❑ Cape May Warbler
- ❑ Black-throated Blue Warbler
- ❑ Yellow-rumped Warbler

- ❏ Black-throated Gray Warbler
- ❏ Black-throated Green Warbler
- ❏ Townsend's Warbler
- ❏ Blackburnian Warbler
- ❏ Yellow-throated Warbler
- ❏ Pine Warbler
- ❏ Kirtland's Warbler
- ❏ Prairie Warbler
- ❏ Palm Warbler
- ❏ Bay-breasted Warbler
- ❏ Blackpoll Warbler
- ❏ Cerulean Warbler
- ❏ Black-and-white Warbler
- ❏ American Redstart
- ❏ Prothonotary Warbler
- ❏ Worm-eating Warbler
- ❏ Swainson's Warbler
- ❏ Ovenbird
- ❏ Northern Waterthrush
- ❏ Louisiana Waterthrush
- ❏ Kentucky Warbler
- ❏ Connecticut Warbler
- ❏ Mourning Warbler
- ❏ Common Yellowthroat
- ❏ Hooded Warbler
- ❏ Wilson's Warbler
- ❏ Canada Warbler
- ❏ Yellow-breasted Chat
- ❏ Summer Tanager
- ❏ Scarlet Tanager
- ❏ Western Tanager
- ❏ Green-tailed Towhee
- ❏ Spotted Towhee
- ❏ Eastern Towhee
- ❏ Bachman's Sparrow
- ❏ American Tree Sparrow
- ❏ Chipping Sparrow
- ❏ Clay-colored Sparrow
- ❏ Field Sparrow
- ❏ Vesper Sparrow
- ❏ Lark Sparrow
- ❏ Black-throated Sparrow
- ❏ Lark Bunting
- ❏ Savannah Sparrow
- ❏ Grasshopper Sparrow
- ❏ Henslow's Sparrow
- ❏ Le Conte's Sparrow
- ❏ Nelson's Sharp-tailed Sparrow
- ❏ Saltmarsh Sharp-tailed Sparrow
- ❏ Seaside Sparrow
- ❏ Fox Sparrow
- ❏ Song Sparrow
- ❏ Lincoln's Sparrow
- ❏ Swamp Sparrow
- ❏ White-throated Sparrow
- ❏ Harris's Sparrow
- ❏ White-crowned Sparrow
- ❏ Dark-eyed Junco
- ❏ Lapland Longspur
- ❏ Chestnut-collared Longspur
- ❏ Snow Bunting
- ❏ Northern Cardinal
- ❏ Rose-breasted Grosbeak
- ❏ Black-headed Grosbeak
- ❏ Blue Grosbeak
- ❏ Lazuli Bunting
- ❏ Indigo Bunting
- ❏ Painted Bunting
- ❏ Dickcissel
- ❏ Bobolink
- ❏ Red-winged Blackbird
- ❏ Eastern Meadowlark
- ❏ Yellow-headed Blackbird
- ❏ Rusty Blackbird
- ❏ Brewer's Blackbird
- ❏ Common Grackle
- ❏ Boat-tailed Grackle
- ❏ Shiny Cowbird
- ❏ Brown-headed Cowbird
- ❏ Orchard Oriole
- ❏ Bullock's Oriole
- ❏ Baltimore Oriole
- ❏ Brambling
- ❏ Pine Grosbeak
- ❏ Purple Finch
- ❏ House Finch
- ❏ Red Crossbill
- ❏ White-winged Crossbill
- ❏ Common Redpoll
- ❏ Hoary Redpoll
- ❏ Pine Siskin
- ❏ American Goldfinch
- ❏ Evening Grosbeak
- ❏ House Sparrow

Index